Teaching Your Children to TELL THEMSELVES THE TRUTH

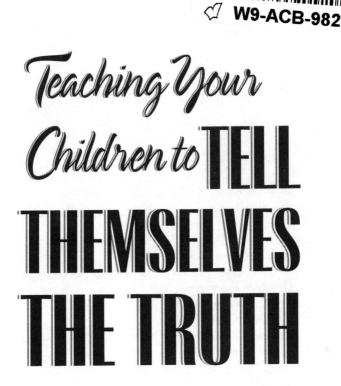

Books by Dr. Backus

Empowering Parents
    (with Candace Backus)
Finding the Freedom of Self-Control
Finding the Freedom of Self-Control Study Guide
    (with Steven Wiese)
The Good News About Worry
The Hidden Rift With God
The Paranoid Prophet
Teaching Your Children to Tell Themselves the Truth
    (with Candace Backus)
Telling Each Other the Truth
Telling the Truth to Troubled People
Telling Yourself the Truth (with Marie Chapian)
Telling Yourself the Truth Study Guide
    (with Marie Chapian)
Untwisting Twisted Relationships
    (with Candace Backus)
Untwisting Twisted Relationships Study Guide
    (with Candace Backus)
What Did I Do Wrong? What Can I Do Now?
    (with Candace Backus)
Why Do I Do What I Don't Want to Do?
    (with Marie Chapian)

Tapes by Dr. Backus

Taking Charge of Your Emotions
Telling Each Other the Truth
Telling Yourself the Truth

Teaching Your Children to TELL THEMSELVES THE TRUTH

William & Candace BACKUS

BETHANY HOUSE PUBLISHERS
MINNEAPOLIS, MINNESOTA 55438

Published by Bethany House Publishers
A Ministry of Bethany Fellowship, Inc.
6820 Auto Club Road, Minneapolis, Minnesota 55438

Printed in the United States of America

Library of Congress Cataloging-in-Publication Data

Backus, William D.
    Teaching your children to tell themselves the truth / William & Candace Backus.
        p.   cm.
1. Child rearing—Religious aspects—Christianity.
2. Truthfulness and falsehood in Children. I. Backus, Candace.
    II. Title.
BV4529.B27   1992
649'.7—dc20
ISBN 1–55661–279–6
                                          92–30635
                                          CIP

To Kathy & Kirstie

Teaching & Learning the Truth Together

WILLIAM and CANDACE BACKUS live in Forest Lake, Minnesota. They serve as counselors at the Center for Christian Psychological Services, St. Paul. Candace is Vice President of Minnesota Psychtests, Inc. William is a clinical psychologist and assistant pastor of a large Lutheran church.

Contents

Introduction

Walking in Truth

"Sometimes I almost wish I didn't have children," Polly murmured.

"What's the problem? Kids out of control?" asked her counselor.

"Oh no! They're wonderful. Really. I enjoy every minute with them. But I can't let myself even *think* about the kind of world they're going to face when they grow up. How can I prepare them for all the struggle of adult life—let alone the evil that's ahead?

Polly isn't the only parent haunted by the frightening images of a rapidly changing world. Kids can watch thousands of murders a year in their own living rooms on TV; adolescents have been known to kill each other over a pair of shoes; and metal detectors are the latest "educational innovation" in many schools. Child-care training for single mothers and instruction in the use of condoms are required classes in some high schools.

Students today are in desperate need of a few "Thou shalt not's"—but they're not likely to get them in the classroom. The Supreme Court banned discussion of the Ten Commandments from public schools. Instead, courses in values-clarification teach children to identify their own values, implying that a child's own ideas of right and wrong, no matter where they come from, are as good as any others. Yes, values are important. But values based on lies and misconceptions are worse than no values at all. For values to be truly valuable in our families and in our society, they must be founded on truth.

All around us we see human personalities destroyed by an evil spiritual power that feeds itself and its own disastrous aims on deception and suppressing the truth! "For the devil wished to live according to himself when he did not abide in the Truth. The souce of man's happiness lies only in God."[1]

"But how can I make a difference for my children? What on earth can I do to equip them for survival in a crumbling culture?" Polly wanted to know. And so do most parents who are aware of what is happening to their children in today's world!

Many Christians have long been aware that deception on a grand scale is responsible for the trouble. Doesn't it seem reasonable, then, that the remedy is to teach children to tell themselves the truth? But what is truth? Where do we find it? And how can we use truth to help our children evaluate experience, solve problems, express themselves effectively, and behave appropriately?

Some computers remain locked until the user types in a password. The computer demands that the user have a right to operate the machine. The computer program acts as a sort of guard at the gate. Like a sentry, it prevents unauthorized users from entering and doing damage. Socrates, Augustine, and other careful thinkers taught that God has built something similar into human creatures, enabling us to recognize the truth when we see it. "Otherwise," reasoned Socrates, "how could we ever identify the truth when we came across it?" Do you sometimes get the feeling that what you are reading or hearing simply has to be true? Have certain truths of Scripture commended themselves to you even when you had no independent evidence? At those times, you may have experienced the operation of God's built-in gate guard recognizing truth and allowing it to pass. We think even children have such a gatekeeper, so that they can often recognize the truth when they hear it. It is certain that those people who have come to faith and received the indwelling Holy Spirit can recognize the truth. Jesus promised that the Holy Spirit would live in His disciples and perform precisely that function.[2]

What will the truth do? Truth can "rustproof" you and your offspring against the corrosive notions now eating like acid through the human spirit and soul. If your children learn to know and walk in the truth, they can live safely above the decaying rot that so frightens sensitive parents today.

What Is Truth?

The word *truth* has been utterd so thoughtlessly for so long that people now use it to mean anything they want someone else to believe, regardless of the evidence. "I'm telling you the truth," said the father to his teenage son. "I'd really like to go to your game, but I have to work tonight." When the son came home after his game, he learned that his father didn't work after all. He'd gotten a call from a friend requesting help on a building project and had dashed right over to help. The next time this father tried to teach his son a Christian principle he believed to be important, he couldn't figure out why the boy did not believe him. The answer is simply that this man's words did not match his actions.

The surest way to live happily and successfully is to get ourselves into harmony with the truth. For the Christian it is important to begin with four foundational statements about truth:

First, truth is a person. Jesus had a great deal to say about truth, and one statement in particular stands out. He said, "I am . . . the truth" (John 14:6). Jesus didn't mean simply that He was *telling* the truth, though of course He never lied. He meant that all truth resides in Him. His words don't merely *reflect* the way things are; His words *make* things the way they are. When He calls water wine, the water must blush and become real wine. When He says, "Let there be light," the darkness must disappear.

Jesus is the Truth because He is God coming true to all His words and promises. "For all the promises of God find their 'Yes' in Him."[3] So, in Jesus, the Truth is a Person. That is the basis of all other truth. The first step in teaching children to tell themselves the truth consists of introducing them to Jesus, the Truth in Person.

Second, truth is the Word about Jesus. This idea is easier for us to grasp because we generally think of truth as something expressed in language. Truth is the message about Jesus. His life and work are God's promises coming true. In Him, God does what He has said He would do.

Third, truth is the book containing the messsage of Jesus, God's Truth in Person. The Bible was written by authors inspired by God, and it is without falsehood or error. In one way, it is similar to the Government Bureau of Standards, which keeps official weights and measures. We can test the accuracy of a measuring device by comparing it to the one kept by this government office. If a sack of sugar weighing a pound on my scale does not weigh a pound on the government's scale, my scale is inaccurate. In the same way, the Bible is the standard against which we test statements purporting to be true. If a statement contradicts the Bible, it cannot be true.

Fourth, truth is what our reason and senses tell us. From the Bible we learn that God created an orderly, predictable world that we can perceive through our five senses. Over the past thirty years, however, it has become fashionable to believe that truth is subjective, that people can create their own reality, that there is no need to rely on empirical evidence. People believe that by defining their own truth they will gain ultimate freedom; what they gain instead is doubt and skepticism.

The truths we talk about in this book have to do with all four of these aspects. God's truth expressed through His Word and through His Son, Jesus, settles the truth about our value to Him and tells us how we should relate to others. And God's truth expressed in creation enables us to evaluate our experiences because we know that the world is predictable.

People say things that are not true; circumstances arise that are easy to misinterpret; and outright lies flood our society. For children to survive this cultural chaos, they must learn to cut to the heart of every matter and find the core of truth in what they hear, what they feel, and what they observe.

Where to Find Truth

The Bible will save us from the lies so rampant in our culture if we listen to and obey its teachings. God has spoken a Word we can trust. We know it is absolute and unchanging for three reasons. First, it comes from God himself, who never lies. Second, God backed it up with evidence: the resurrection of Christ from the dead; convincing testimony of credible witnesses; and astounding changes in the behavior of believers. Third, God gave us His Holy Spirit who enables us to recognize and believe God's truth when we hear it. (See John 14:25; 15:26; 16:12–15.) People who have come to faith and have received the indwelling Holy Spirit can recognize the truth. Jesus promised that the Holy Spirit would live in His disciples and perform precisely that function. (See 1 Corinthians 2:6–16.) We may make errors in determining truth; we're not infallible and many external factors are working to influence us. But we have the resources to help us work through puzzling data and find God's truth.

How Can We Use This Truth With Our Children?

Some of you have already been introduced to the idea of wholeness through truth. You may even have studied and applied the principles in *Telling Yourself the Truth*.[4] If you have witnessed dramatic changes in your own life as you developed the habit of replacing wrong beliefs with positive self-talk, you may want to teach the same principles to your children. Although the contemporary world has obscured this fact to some extent, you and all parents were meant to be teachers of your own offspring. God said it in so many words: "These words which I command you this day shall be upon your heart; and you shall teach them diligently to your children. . . ."[5]

Emotional, relational, and other kinds of hardships eventually come to all children. These pressures are generally greater today than when we were growing up. But there are coping tools available now that we knew nothing about in our childhood years. As parents, you can teach your children how to maintain truthful self-talk, one of the basic needs for having a healthy spiritual life.

The idea of understanding and working to modify a child's cognitions is a new one. What we have discovered in our research is that to teach children to tell themselves the truth, we must consider the child's entire life-span. A child's entire life is intricate. What he learns at an early age, he will carry into adulthood with him. Therefore our goal must be to teach children the truth while they are young. Most parents want their children to surpass them, and to become more competent, more truthful, better adjusted, and happier. It follows then that we will want to help them apply the truth better than we did too.

By working through the chapters ahead, you can help your children learn the truth and use it to shape their lives. The book is a simple, easy to follow, sequenced plan with plenty of examples and ideas for teaching specific age groups. Each chapter builds on the previous one and presumes the next, so you will want to read the book in its entirety.

This book can be used to instruct one child at a time or a whole neighborhood full of kids. Apply these teachings to your specific situation however you wish. As you work with your children, you can learn to apply truth in your own life as well.

And, of course, practice makes perfect! Encourage your

children frequently in what they are learning. This will take both time and patience, but it will be more than worthwhile when you see your children begin to comprehend and apply truth in their own lives.

1

Finding Out What Children Tell Themselves

Stop, Look, and Listen to What Children Don't Say

By age thirteen Lori was suffering bouts of anxiety so severe that she refused to go to school, visit friends, or even go shopping unless her mother went along. Lori's anxiety, which had developed over a period of years, began after a devastating life blow. Her father, whom she dearly loved, left home when Lori was five and never returned.

As Lori grew older, her anxiety about being left alone made life increasingly awkward and difficult for both her and her mother. It was clear that if Lori did not solve her problem, she would become an emotionally handicapped adult.

For several years Lori's mother did nothing to discourage her daughter's clingy behavior. The abrupt departure of Lori's father had been as devastating to Martha, Lori's mother, as it had been to Lori; and Lori's dependency gave Martha a welcome sense of being needed.

When Lori became a teenager, however, Martha realized that her daughter's behavior was not healthy, so she came to us for help. We encouraged her to talk about her feelings for her mother. Martha had always been flattered that Lori wanted to spend so much time with her, but when the truth started to emerge, Martha saw a darker reality. Lori's attachment stemmed not from affection but from *fear*. And her fear resulted from a few totally false statements she was telling herself.

In their first counseling sessions, Lori and Bill had the following chat. Please note now Lori gradually gets into the conversation even though the sessions were arranged by her mother—an arrangement guaranteed to elicit stubborn resistance from some adolescents. Please note how Lori reveals the deeper layers of thinking that contain her misbeliefs. Why did she open up to Bill when she hadn't told her mother the truth about how she felt? Perhaps she had felt considerable pressure from Mom to perform differently, while Bill, unlike her mother, didn't begin with a demand that she "go to school" or "get a boyfriend." Not that parents don't need to urge their children to act normally. It's just that sometimes it's easier for a child to talk with someone who doesn't have "administrative" responsibilities for the child's actions.

BILL: I'm not sure whether coming in here was your own idea or not, Lori.

LORI: No way! My mom was the one who thought I should talk to somebody. It wasn't my idea. No way!

BILL: Then maybe I should be talking to your mother.

LORI: Well, I don't think she . . . I mean, she doesn't know what the problem is. She thinks I don't like other kids, and I do. She's all worried about what she calls my "social development."

BILL: Your social development?

LORI: She calls it that. What bothers her is that I hang around home a lot and I kinda want to know where she is all the time.

BILL: Your mom doesn't want to tell you where she's going?

LORI: No, it's not that, it's just that she thinks I worry more than I should. She says it's not normal for a kid to worry so much.

BILL: What does she mean by "worry"—what do you *do?*

LORI: Well, maybe I am too nervous about things. I stay home from school a lot and that really gets to Mom. She's afraid I won't graduate or get into college or anything. She tries to make me go to school and go shopping without her and stuff like that. She complains because I don't have a boyfriend. She criticizes me for never going anywhere with other kids. I guess I am uptight about some stuff. I probably do need to calm down more.

BILL: Have you been able to notice what makes you "nervous" or "uptight"? Can you tell what kinds of things bring on those feelings?

LORI: Oh, sure. Being away from home. Being away from my mom. Being in school or any place new. It's not that I don't like other kids, really it's not. It's just that I get all jittery and tense when I don't know for sure where Mom is, and sometimes even if I know where she is I get that way because I know I can't get to her fast.

BILL: I see. It seems to have to do with your mother—with being too far away from her?

LORI: Yeah, it seems to. It seems like I worry about her too. Like I'm afraid something's going to happen.

BILL: To her?

LORI: Uh-huh, like somebody's going to hurt her or kidnap her—take her away—kill her—something. When I'm not with her these thoughts go through my head and I can't get rid of them until I see her again. It's like dumb, I know, but it doesn't help to know I shouldn't worry like this because I do worry anyway.

BILL: Do you ever think about what you'd do or what would happen to you if your mom did die or something?

LORI: I guess I don't think that far ahead. I get so scared just imagining it ... (breaks off—cries). Like I'd probably die myself of ... (breaks off again—more tears). What *would* happen to me? I wouldn't have anybody—not anybody! I'd be left alone with no one to take care of me. I guess I just couldn't think *what* to do.

BILL: So you think if you're not with her all the time, you could lose your mother some way?

LORI: I guess that's why I get so worried and uptight whenever I try to be away from her. I guess I think it'd be just like with my father.

BILL: Your father?

LORI: He moved out when I was little. I've always been afraid Mom would go too, I guess—or if she didn't, something might happen to take her away anyhow—and I'd be left completely alone.

BILL: So you stick pretty close to her to try to make sure you don't lose her like you lost your dad? To try to make sure you won't be left completely alone? That you won't end up with nobody to care for you or to love you?

LORI: Yeah, that seems right.

BILL: And you can't spend time with friends or have a boyfriend because you have to stick around your mother just to make sure?

LORI: Right. And that's why I worry so much about having to go to school. All day, when I do go, I'm tense and worried, and I can't wait to get home.

By the end of the interview, Lori showed diminished tension just from this brief interaction, probably because even as she verbalized her fears (for the first time ever, it turned out), she began to see a glimmer of the light of truth shining on her misbeliefs. Bill went on to "make a treatment contract" with Lori. He told her the work would involve facing her misbeliefs and changing them to do away with much of her fear and worry. He also made it clear that Lori would be required to work on her separation misbeliefs by actually separating from her mother, for brief periods at first, then for gradually longer periods while she learned to tell herself the truth. Although the very thought scared her, Lori agreed to do her best to get well, even if it meant putting up with some discomfort for a while, because she wanted to be free.

What were Lori's misbeliefs? You can probably guess from what you have read. She believed that:

- Her mother would leave her, just as her father had, or die.
- Her father's leaving her proved he didn't love her, and if her mother left she wouldn't have any love at all.
- If anything happened to her mother, she herself would not survive, so hanging on to Mom was her first and most important priority in life.
- She must stay close to her mother, because by doing so she could prevent the loss.
- It was risky for her to go to school or to spend time with her friends because she might lose her mother if she wasn't at Mom's side.

In later sessions, Bill asked Lori to look at these notions and ask herself whether they were true. Lori began to realize, as she faced the issues head on for the first time, that the truth was clearly something other than what she had been telling herself. The chance of her mother's sudden death was extremely *slight*, for Mom was in good health and only thirty-eight! Similarly, there was no indication whatever that Lori's mother might leave her. Mothers don't just up and desert their kids. Had she ever known a mother to leave children, especially after their father had left the home? Never once. Even if her mother *should* die or disappear (utterly unlikely though these events were), Lori's maternal grandparents loved her dearly and would take her in gladly. She would feel bad, of course, but she absolutely would not starve or lack loving care. Finally, Lori's constant presence wouldn't prevent her mother's sudden death anyway. Nor would it keep her mother from leaving if she should decide to do so. Going to school or spending time with friends couldn't possibly increase the likelihood that Lori would lose her mom.

In addition, Bill and Lori devised graded "separation-from-Mom" exercises—easy, short, not-too-distant separation experiences at first (like spending short periods in the shopping center alone while Mom waited in the parking lot), then more difficult, longer-lasting, farther-away sep-arations (like staying with an aunt and uncle who lived three hundred miles away) later. These exercises helped Lori to actually experience the truth that she could safely be separated from her mother.

Of course all of this took time, but it worked. Lori came to know that her fears were unfounded, unhealthy, and needlessly counterproductive. Of course it took several months of patient effort before Lori was able to experience complete freedom, but she *started* to improve the moment she began telling herself the truth and doing her exercises.

Lori was not able to tell herself the truth after only one or two counseling sessions. It took several months before she was able to answer questions on the basis of evidence rather than intuition. And it was several more months be-fore she started to see the discrepancy between what she knew and the way she behaved.

Eventually, Lori did learn to replace her misbeliefs with truth, face her fears as paper tigers, and find her freedom! For four years, she has been freer to enjoy her life as a high-school student, with a strong personal esteem and a grow-ing Christian faith.

What's Going On in There?

The natural tendency of parents is to focus on a child's irritating behavior and to look for ways to change it. How can I get Janie to do her homework? or, How can I get Rick to stop picking fights? Frustrated parents want to know. How can we help Jane with her depression? What can we do for Gary—he's so afraid to go to school.

Parents must learn to read their children in two ways: through what they say and through what they do. Martha had to read Lori's behavior because Lori herself had never learned to focus on her thoughts and fears. They had started when she was too young to even identify them, much less put them into words. And over the years they had become so much a part of her that she could not think of herself apart from them.

Some children may verbalize their though'
but frequently, due to lack of experience, thei'
situation has serious flaws. For example,
make comments similar to the following may be
assessing a situation and in need of someone to help u.
tell themselves the truth:

> "My teacher made me read out loud in class again
> today. She always picks on me."
> "I hate everybody in my whole class. They always
> make fun of me."
> "I'm the stupidest kid in my whole math class."
> "Patty invited everybody but me to her party. No-
> body ever invites me to anything."

Children who frequently express emotional pain exhibit
self-esteem problems, and those who make excuses for bad
behavior may have a faulty view of reality because they have
not been telling themselves the truth. Parents can help children overcome this emotional disability by finding out what
their kids are telling themselves, showing them how to determine whether or not what they are telling themselves is
truthful, helping them to see contradictions between reality
and perception, and then encouraging them to act on what
they have learned.

2

Eavesdropping on a Child's Self-Talk

What Does Your Child Believe About Events?

Judy, age seven, had not played with her grandmother for most of Grandma's visit. Her five-year-old brother, Jeff, cornered Grandma for a game of *Candyland* while Judy kept herself busy drawing pictures. Now bath time, the precursor of bedtime, had arrived. When Judy's mother asked her if she would rather bathe tonight or tomorrow morning, Judy replied that she would wait until morning. She explained that she wanted to finish a picture for Grandpa. So Jeff climbed into the tub, delighted to let Grandma scrub his back and wash his hair.

Soon it was time for bed, and Grandma got ready to leave. "But I want to take a bath now!" Judy demanded.

"Sorry, honey," Mom replied, "it's time for bed now. You can take your bath tomorrow."

"I want to take a bath now!" Judy wailed. Soon she was screaming, tears running down her cheeks. But her mother remained firm, so Judy had to go to bed without her bath. She had made a choice, and it was too late to change her mind. Her mournful sobs continued after the light was turned out.

What caused Judy's outburst?

To understand her tantrum, we have to understand her thoughts. We often call key thoughts *self-talk*. This internal conversation grows out of what children believe. These beliefs can determine whether they feel good or bad and even what they will do and will not do. Beliefs and self-talk decide emotions and issue the cues for behavior.

Judy may have told herself several things based on her beliefs:

> "I can take my bath now that I've finished Grandpa's picture. It's only fair, because Jeff got to take his bath."
>
> "It's not fair that I don't get some time to play with Grandma."
>
> "I want to make up my own mind, not always be told what to do."
>
> "It's terrible that Mom won't let me take a bath now when I want one so much—and when I want time with Grandma."

Thoughts, Feelings, and Actions

To understand how thoughts cause feelings and actions, imagine a little booth in the child's brain furnished with one tiny chair. On the chair sits a diminutive figure who does absolutely nothing but talk and/or show pictures. This figure talks night and day, sometimes projecting images instead of putting the thoughts into words. The words and images are the thoughts that stimulate responses such as feelings and actions, moods and habits.

The writers of Scripture and our Lord declared that what people believe will either save or ruin them. Our clinical experience has repeatedly borne witness to this biblical truth. (See Matthew 8:13; Mark 16:16; John 20:31; Romans 9:33; 1 John 4:1. These passages represent a tiny fragment of the New Testament material on the centrality of what you believe and, of course, tell yourself.) That belief is crucial for children, as it was one of Jesus' own lessons (cf. Mark 9:42).

Her Thoughts Are Not Your Thoughts

"I don't understand Judy," her mother murmured. "She's so rebellious!"

From the moment children enter this world, their behavior defies adult understanding. Impulses dominate the minds of eighteen-month-olds, and they act on every one of them. That is the only option for young children, because action alone releases inner tensions. Young children don't see the future. And they often forget the past and the punishment they received for an impulsive action the day before yesterday. For them, the present is the major reality.

Four-year-olds often believe the closet is crammed with pernicious ghosts. Why? Because toddlers aren't mature enough intellectually to tell themselves that imagination is one thing and the truth, reality, is another. So you can see why four-year-olds can have night terrors, and why they sometimes make up stories about monsters and goblins.

At ages five and six, children are developing consciences. Prior to that, they have no norms or customs integrated into their belief systems. Until they make beliefs their own, they will not automatically tell themselves, as adults do, "This is wrong. That is right. If I do this, I'll feel guilty. If I do that, I'll be proud of myself."

By nine or ten, children begin to incorporate the self-talk of their peer groups. Now the attitudes and beliefs of other kids become their own. So their self-talk will be psychologically separate from their parents' adult self-talk.

The biochemical changes taking place in a thirteen-year-old will accompany self-talk that elicits sullenness, anger, and depression. Remember—when chemistry goes awry, a youngster's self-talk changes, too. Chemical changes touch thoughts and feelings, not merely the state of a person's body. Through all the changes from babyhood to adulthood, children are building their beliefs.

How Kids Generate Wrong Beliefs

Learning. Some wrong beliefs are learned—from words spoken by parents, other adults, or other kids. One child overheard her aunt confiding to her mother that shaking hands with the undertaker who attended her church "gave her the creeps because he handles all those dead bodies." The child took notice, because her best friend was the funeral director's daughter! From that day on, she avoided her friend. From one casual remark of an aunt, this child had picked up some destructive and erroneous beliefs. She told herself she would feel creepy if she played with her friend, and her feelings fell into line.

Modeling. Other erroneous beliefs come from observing and copying the actions of others, a process called *modeling*. A boy's belief in the inferiority of women can come from observing the disdainful manner in which his father treats his mother. From watching father, such a youngster can come to believe that his mother and all women must be of small account.

Deduction and Reasoning. Children deduce many false notions. Certain errors of logic may occur during deduction so that the individual distorts the truth in specific ways.

Logical Misbelief

Dr. Aaron T. Beck has labeled some common errors of logic in erroneous inferences, and most of these errors are seen in children as well as adults:

Dichotomous Thinking. Children with this thinking pattern divide everything into two categories—either totally bad or totally good, pitch black or snow white, perfect or awful. "I'm never going to get an A in math," says the eighth-grader, "and I can't handle getting a B. I'm a loser for sure." This student's thoughts put things in paired categories: perfect or intolerable; but in reality most things come in infinite gradations.

Over-generalization. Here children create a general rule, usually negative, proving things must be awful. Seldom do they over-generalize from one or two positive events to the conclusion that things are just fine. A young teen applies for a job as a stock boy at the local hardware store. If he doesn't get it, he contacts the local newspaper about an opening for a carrier. If he fails to get either job, he concludes, "I probably can't get a job. Obviously, nobody wants me. No way will I have any spending money. I might as well give up!" The young person has put himself into a dark funk by believing, based on one or two experiences, that his search for work is hopeless.

Disregarding the Affirmative. In this kind of thinking, children use *cynicism* and *negativism* as the means by which they assess life. Thus they decide that any good that happens doesn't count, that any success is an accident, an exception which only proves the rule. A high-school student may say, "I know I got A's in history and English, but the English teacher likes me and history's easy. I'm no good in school and I'd never make it through college if I went."

Arbitrary Inference. For no good reason, a youngster may assign an unfavorable meaning to circumstances or outcomes. Take the case of the twelve-year-old who has moved to a new neighborhood and a new school. The other seventh-graders have known one another for years, but the newcomer finds herself excluded from the "in" group, forced to spend her free time alone or hobnobbing with younger, lower-status youngsters. "What is wrong with me?" she may ask herself. She examines every detail of her face in the mirror. Ruminating about her unpopularity, she finally concludes, "I must be a creep. There must be something about me that is revolting to other people. I don't like myself at all. I wish I could stay home from school or go live far away in the mountains!"

Magnification. Children sometimes make themselves believe that things they don't like are major disasters. If parents force these types of children to wear clothes they don't like, their self-talk turns a minor matter into major abuse. "Mom's making me wear my jacket. I'll be too hot. Nobody else is wearing a jacket. It's awful! It's just not fair!"

Minimization. In this case children make certain events mean little or nothing, unrealistically diminishing them until they're insignificant. A preschooler draws a picture, but when her father praises her for it, she says, "It's not a very good house. My friend did a better one. And if you like it, it's only because you're my daddy!"

Replace Kids' Wrong Beliefs With the Truth

Judy's outburst over her bath grew out of her wrong beliefs. Understanding a child's beliefs is the first step toward understanding behavior, but parents must walk further with their children. They must replace wrong beliefs with the truth because truth will set their children free. And in this freedom they will find wholeness.

3

Entering Your Child's World

Telling Your Children the Truth About Themselves

Mitch's mother did her best to help her son develop high self-esteem. Starting when he was just an infant she took advantage of every opportunity to tell him how superior, intelligent, and handsome he was and that he could have anything and everything he wanted out of life. Mitch believed her, and he set life goals based on her assessment. In high school he determined that he would marry the prettiest girl in the world, make his first million by age thirty, and retire before he was forty to live the life of ease and fun to which the virtue of his superior gifts entitled him.

People who knew Mitch in high school would have said that his mother's tactics worked. He was willing to try everything, and he excelled at much of what he tried. The teachers and other students liked him. He studied hard and got good grades. He was a member of the Honor Society, student government, the basketball team, was captain of the debate team, played first-chair trombone in the orchestra, and still found time to be active in his church and youth group.

His mother was pleased that she had been so successful in building her son's self-image.

But she did not limit herself to saying positive things about Mitch's achievements and character. In addition to her frequent affirmations, she made excuses when Mitch came through with a less-than-perfect performance. If he got anything other than an A on a test or paper, she told him it was because his teacher was having a bad day. She always blamed something other than Mitch for his failure, no matter how small. When Mitch lost the election for senior-class president, his mother assured him, "Sally only won because she flirts with all the boys and because it's the 'in' thing to vote for a girl. But you would have made a better president." Mitch believed everything his mother told him because he had no good reason not to.

Then came his first major disappointment. He was not accepted at the college of his choice, the college he'd dreamed of attending all through high school. He had been so sure that he would get in that he hadn't even applied anywhere else, so at the last minute he had to scramble to get in to another school.

From then on the myth that Mitch's mom had built around her son crumbled rapidly. He tried out for basketball, but didn't make the team—not even second string. There were no openings in the orchestra, so he tried out for band but wound up getting only third chair. Without his mother around to pump him up and make excuses for his failures, Mitch became depressed. His roommate only scoffed at his depression. "Welcome to the real world, pal," was the extent of the sympathy Mitch got from him.

Mitch tried to use his mother's tactics on himself. He rationalized that he wasn't chosen simply because he was new and no one knew him. He just needed to prove himself. If he worked hard everyone would realize that they had made a mistake in judgment and he would be chosen second semester. Besides, he reasoned, this would give him more time to concentrate on his studies, so maybe it was all for the best.

This line of thinking got Mitch through the first few months of college. Even with the extra study time, however, his grades on tests and papers weren't as good as he thought they should be. And when he received his first-semester grades, he was devastated. He didn't even make the dean's list. When his mother asked how he did, he lied. Lying to his mother made him feel awful; he had never lied to her before. But he couldn't bring himself to tell her the truth. He knew the disappointment would be too much for her. It still hadn't dawned on him that his mother had been lying to him for years.

Mitch's mother thought she could help her son develop good self-esteem by being less than truthful with him, but she was wrong. Although she had helped him develop *high* self-esteem, it was neither good nor healthy because it was faulty; it was based on lies, not truth. The other thing Mitch's mom helped her son develop was dishonesty. Because she neglected to tell him the truth for so many years, he is now unable to tell her the truth.

Some dictionaries and authors define self-esteem as a *good* opinion of self or a *high* evaluation of self. But since the word "esteem" comes originally from Latin words meaning "estimate" (either good or bad), esteem can mean no more than evaluation. By our definition, therefore, self-esteem has nothing to do with having a high opinion of one's abilities. Instead, it refers to a person's beliefs about him/herself—whether negative or positive. We use the term in this neutral sense so we can speak of poor self-esteem, negative self-esteem, and false self-esteem, as well as their opposites.

Poor self-esteem is an untruthful, or false, set of beliefs about oneself. Many characters in literature and throughout history have exhibited unrealistic positive beliefs about themselves. Raskolnikov, in Dostoyevsky's *Crime and Punishment*, believed he was a superman who could kill without guilt. Narcissus, in Greek mythology, fell hopelessly in love with his own beauty. Pooh Bah, in the opera *The Mikado*, sings comically about his "family pride." Absalom, rebellious and proud, led the attack against his father, King David. Adolph Hitler and Joseph Stalin slaughtered millions of innocent people to achieve their selfish, warped desires. These and other well-known names are synonymous with the deadly sin of pride in one of its many forms.

What troubles us is that some of these evils are mistaken by the undiscerning for healthy self-esteem.

But the low self-esteem that is the target of the current wave of "self-esteem correction" manifests itself in pessimism, poor performance, discouragement, depression, and a generally down-at-the-heels attitude toward life. Those suffering from it use self-abasing, inaccurate, over-generalized, and negative terms to evaluate themselves.

Unfortunately, the correction for this faulty thinking simply substitutes one set of falsehoods for another. Standing in front of a mirror and proclaiming ourselves uniquely stupendous violates the biblical injunction to not think more highly of ourselves than we ought to think, but to think [of ourselves] soberly (Romans 12:3).

Even *Newsweek* magazine, in its February 17, 1992 cover story, sharply criticized the trendy emphasis on self-esteem. It has gone too far, according to the *Newsweek* authors, when adults enthusiastically reward children for failures as well as for successes to promote *self-esteem*.

And Christians, steeped in biblical injunctions to cultivate honesty, humility, and lowliness, have problems accepting the contention that psychological wholeness is the same as an unwaveringly affirmative self-image.

Because people can think more highly of themselves than the truth warrants, they can have self-esteem that is poor even if it is high. Mitch had high self-esteem, but it wasn't good because it was based on faulty beliefs.

Betty's Mistake

Betty was upset because her children came home from Sunday school saying that their teacher had told them they were sinful.

"I'm not sure an idea like that fits in with a healthy self-image," Betty complained to her pastor the following week.

The pastor tried to explain to Betty that undiluted self-approval can turn a human being into a monster. "We could all become healthier," he said, "by occasionally facing the unpleasant truth about ourselves. We all exhibit negative behavior at one time or another. If we don't admit that, there's no basis for repentance and no hope for forgiveness."

But Betty had come to accept the popular notion that children should learn only self-affirming ideas, so she took her children to another Sunday school.

Good self-esteem cannot come from hearing only one-sided information about ourselves, even if the one side is positive. It does not harm children to raise them to face the truths that they are sinners—that they sometimes do wrong unintentionally and sometimes willfully. If children accept this and learn to appreciate their positive traits as well as acknowledge the not-so-positive ones, the result is good self-esteem, even though some self-judgments are negative.

Luther taught a concept that all Christian parents should adopt as part of their philosophy of parenting: Christian believers are *simul justus et peccator*—"at the same time righteous and sinful." Parents can honestly teach their believing offspring this simple truth.

When the apostle Paul pronounced himself "chief of sinners" (1 Timothy 1:15), he was exhibiting good self-esteem—good because his statement revealed an accurate self-evaluation. David, in Psalm 51, wrote: "Surely I have been a sinner from birth, sinful from the time my mother conceived me" (v. 5). Though negative, his statement was accurate and therefore qualifies as good self-esteem. David's comment in the next verse confirms the idea that godly self-esteem—an esteem that comes from knowing our position under God and in relation to others—is something God wants for us: "Surely you desire *truth in the inner parts . . .*" (Psalm 51:6).

What we are trying to get across is that good self-esteem may at times involve *negative* self-evaluation. That is the case when *the truth about oneself happens to be negative at the time.* Good self-esteem is having *truthful* beliefs about self rather than simply *positive* beliefs about self.

Martin's Failure

For the first time in his life, Martin failed a test, and he took it hard. He felt so bad that it affected every area of his life.

Fortunately, Martin's teacher realized something was wrong and had a chat with the boy. He probed deeper into Martin's thoughts and learned that he was telling himself some appalling untruths. When the teacher realized what this had done to Martin's self-esteem, he helped him learn to stop attacking himself and instead tell himself the truth.

Martin was over-generalizing, disregarding the affirmative, and magnifying the negative. (See Dr. Aaron Beck's list of common errors of logic, Chapter 2.) He told himself: "I'm a failure in school because I failed the test" (over-generalizing); "I didn't study enough because I'm a lazy goof-off. I'll never amount to anything in life because I can't do anything right" (disregarding the affirmative); "I'll never recover from this disaster because it's always going to be part of my record" (magnification). Martin handled his poor test grade by attacking himself. In essence, he told himself that he was bad, hopelessly bad. Martin's self-esteem was both untruthful and low because he had disregarded the truth.

Martin didn't need to tell himself positive untruths to regenerate his self-esteem. He needed only to tell himself the truth. And the truth was this: The failure was a fluke. Nothing like it had ever happened before. True, Martin had to take responsibility for not studying, but there was a good reason. His family had moved to a motel for a few days while damage to their home was being repaired and there was no quiet spot where Martin could study.

Nor did Martin need to blame someone else for his poor performance. If he had said, "It was my little sister's fault for making so much noise I couldn't study" or "The teacher was at fault because it was an unfair test," Martin might have had high self-esteem, but it would have been based on blame and rationalization rather than on truth.

Instead, after talking the situation through with his

teacher, Martin acknowledged his failure. When Martin stopped telling himself he was bad, and simply admitted the failure and its consequences, he felt better. Why? Because his self-esteem was once again both truthful and high.

Erika's Achievement

Erika was considered a high achiever by her teachers. She did particularly well in English and speech and had been placed in some advanced classes. After several weeks of preparation and competition during the forensic season, she was chosen to represent her class in the state interpretive-reading contest. There she won second prize!

"Congratulations, Erika! I'm so proud of you," said her mother.

"But I didn't win first prize," replied Erika unhappily. "I only got second!"

"Honey, that's still very impressive. It means you did a super job!" Mom replied, perplexed over her daughter's habit of interpreting her successes negatively.

"I lucked out. I think the judges liked me, that's all. I just don't have what it takes to make first, I guess."

Erika fell silent, but continued to look glum. In her own mind, she was talking to herself like this: "I never make it to the top. Whenever I get a good grade or something it's because other people don't do very well, so I'm the only one who gives a halfway decent performance. Or else, some teacher likes me and plays favorites. Teachers usually like me and think I'm good. But I always mess up some way. I'm not that good at much of anything, I guess."

"Tell me what you're thinking, Erika," said her mother softly.

"I tell myself I don't deserve a prize. I'm really no good at this. I deserve to lose because I've fooled my teachers and other people. They think I'm smart, but I'm not," was the girl's response.

People who knew her would be astounded to hear what Erika told herself. With this false set of self-negating automatic thoughts, Erika was making her life miserable. She was an achiever who could never enjoy her successes. Many people express similar sweeping, inaccurate, negative self-evaluations, thereby spoiling any satisfaction they might feel when they do well. Is it any wonder that today's parents are so concerned over their children's self-esteem?

Erika's mother had the good sense to continue the conversation. She went on to show her child what her own self-talk was doing to ruin her successes for her. She taught Erika about what Dr. Beck calls *minimization* (Chapter 2) and paying attention only to *negative* outcomes.

"Erika," she reminded her daughter, "last year when you won the city spelling contest, you said it didn't mean anything because the really good spellers had been accidentally eliminated. Several months ago, Mr. Brighton, the principal, asked you if you would be his student assistant and you said he only asked you because everybody else was too busy. A few weeks ago you got an A on a math test and you said it was because the problems were too easy. Can you see for yourself that you have a habit of downgrading whatever you do?"

"I did say those things, didn't I?" Erika began to let herself consider what her mother was saying. "Maybe you have a point. All those good things couldn't be accidental, I guess. But I always feel like I'm a fake and like I'm really not as good as I seem to people."

"That must not be a very happy feeling, Erika. Can you see now that it comes from what you tell youself? And that what you tell yourself about success comes from your habits of *minimization* and *disregarding the affirmative* rather than from facts?"

Erika listened. She began to realize how irrational it was to regularly judge all her positive outcomes as meaningless while at the same time deciding that any negatives must be the "real truth" about her and her ability. Could she have been listening to the Devil? Of course. Could she learn to tell herself the truth? Could she take off her blinders and see that in reality she sometimes did very well and sometimes (like anyone else) not so well? Yes. She could and she did. And as a result she tasted the freedom truth can bring when a person replaces erroneous self judgments with reality.

Christian parents can make a difference with their children's self-esteem. They can teach their children to soberly and honestly evaluate their behavior and their performance in every area of life.

4

Who's to Blame?

Finding the Truth About Causes

"What difference does it make what caused his problems? I just want him to learn to solve them," grumbled Graham Wood.

His son, Jim, was the subject of our consultation, and we could see that Graham was getting annoyed by our questions. He wanted us to get down to business and tell him how to *fix* Jim instead of worry about history. Jim was an intelligent (much better than average) ninth-grader who, despite his intellectual ability, earned grades that ranged between mediocre and poor. Not only that, Jim went out for ninth-grade baseball and quit after two weeks of practice.

"What can we do with him?" demanded his frustrated father. "All he ever wants to do is sit around and read or play with my computer. He has very few friends, though other kids have called him and asked him to do things with them. We've tried to get him to talk about it, but he just says he doesn't know what's wrong. He says he doesn't care, but I think it's a lie. He mopes a lot."

We weren't really asking about the historical causes of Jim's pattern of failures, though that's how Wood took it.

We had a hunch and we checked it out by interviewing the youngster. He was quite frank and open for a teenager, and his answers confirmed our thoughts.

Jim had a self-talk habit many will recognize. When he hit a home run, Jim assured himself that the homer was an accident. "Everybody connects once in a while," he muttered. Or if he did well on a math test, he reminded himself of the many tests he had done badly on. He knew he wasn't good at math, so his A must have happened by accident.

What he told himself about the math test and the home run followed a pattern. If Jim had a success of any kind, he regularly told himself the success was an accident, due to the good will of others or to some factor totally beyond his control. Whenever something Jim tried worked out poorly, however, he blamed himself. "I'm no good at that." "I never try hard enough." "I never can study right." "I have poor coordination." "I'm no athlete." Jim attributed failures to himself, while the cause of every success he attributed to some outside person, force, or factor utterly beyond his control.

The reason Jim had been performing at such a low level was that he had untruthful self-esteem. It was based on his untruthful self-talk about his own performance and abilities. That self-talk involved a contradiction in thinking. It makes sense that if failure is due to our own actions, then success is also the result of our own efforts. On the other hand, if success is due to external causes beyond our control, then failure also must be due to happenstance rather than our own actions. However, Jim had his thinking all mixed up. He was telling himself the contradictory statement that outside forces caused his success but inner deficiencies caused his failure.

Please bear in mind that in this book *self-esteem* is neutral, referring merely to children's beliefs and self-talk about themselves. Good self-esteem means truthful beliefs and self-talk. All of us have been conditioned to accept the misinformed idea that good self-esteem means thinking highly of ourselves at all times and under all circumstances, whether our behavior is good or bad. It is commonly believed that if children experience a failure or do something wrong, they should be taught to look outside themselves for the cause, while they should learn to attribute all positive outcomes to themselves.

Teaching children to blame others and/or circumstances for negative behaviors but to take credit for all personal success creates moral havoc. Furthermore, teaching children that whatever they do—even if they have a moral, spiritual, or performance failure—is wonderful simply because they are such fine persons can be downright harmful to character development. Positive self-esteem must not be purchased at the expense of personal honesty.

Attribution

What are the *attributional styles* of your children? How do they routinely think about the causes behind their successes? Their failures? Do they habitually attribute their successes to accidental factors, circumstances, someone else's good graces, or to their own hard work and ability? Do they routinely attribute any failures to themselves, their *stupidity*, their *laziness*, or their being *no good* at such things? Or do they habitually take credit for other people's ideas and achievements, attribute success to themselves no matter how much help they have received from God and others, and make clear to everyone that they consider themselves stronger, better, and brighter than everyone else? Do they dwell on their accomplishments? Do they take it as a matter of course that any achievement is solely due to their own excellence, prowess, virtue, or merit? Do they attribute all weakness or failure to circumstances, accidents, other people's interference or persecution, or God's letting them down? In other words, do they assume that when anything goes wrong it cannot be their own fault?

These habitual patterns are called *attributional styles*, and those listed above characterize far too many youngsters today. They are all untruthful and, if unchecked, will lead to self-esteem flaws. They contribute to inaccurate and untruthful (and therefore bad) self-esteem. This is true even if children have high self-esteem.

Truthful Attribution

Psychologists have done considerable research on children's attributional styles. One fact has emerged from this work: Neurotics tend to attribute their successes to the environment, their failures to themselves. So Jim Martin was acting like the neurotic research subjects. No wonder Jim felt miserable about himself.

Like most neurotics, Jim's self-esteem was untruthful. As a result, he made very little effort to succeed in anything, despite his great ability. Why? Well, put yourself in Jim's shoes. If he succeeded in his efforts, he always had to attribute the success to accidental and extraneous factors, so success did not give him the joy of a job well done. Besides that, every effort to do well involved the risk of failure, and Jim felt every failure was due to his own incompetence, regardless of the true circumstances. So failure merely confirmed the boy's painful belief that he didn't have what it took to succeed. Every failure confirmed his self-estimate, "I'm just a loser." No success could offset it because "it just happened that way, I didn't really do it."

Many psychologists suggest teaching children like Jim to cultivate the habit of telling themselves the exact opposite: "I succeeded because I'm good" or "That failure wasn't really mine, it was the fault of the teacher, the coach, the weather, or the textbook's lack of clarity." We disagree with this idea because it disregards the truth to keep self-esteem high. What makes people feel better is not always true.

We believe in objective standards of right and wrong, while some psychologists believe right and wrong are relative, matters of convenience, pragmatics, or opinion. They don't consider another option: truthful attributional style.

The Bible on Self-Esteem and Attribution

Paul's inspired teaching on self-esteem comes through clearly here:

"For by the grace given me I say to every one of you: Do not think of yourself more highly than you ought, but rather think of yourself with sober judgment, in accordance with the measure of faith God has given you" (Romans 12:3). Self-esteem, like all our thoughts, needs to reflect the truth of "sober judgment."

If we care about truth, we will want to help our children develop a *truthful* self-image, *truthful* self-esteem, and a *truthful* attributional style. Parents need to teach children to attribute success and failure to their true causes, insofar as it is possible to know them.

If a student studies hard and earns an A, is it arrogant to take credit? No!

The apostle Paul urges us not to think of ourselves more highly than we ought to think but to think soberly. He doesn't urge us to think we can't do anything right and are no good at all.

When a high-school sprinter trains hard, competes against other good runners, and wins the one-hundred-yard dash, the sprinter shouldn't say, "The only reason I won is that the other guys had an off day."

Both the student and the runner should acknowledge their hard work; otherwise their self-talk is false. Of course, if the student's teacher admits she pumped up the girl's grade because she likes her so much, or if it is clear the sprinter won on a day when the other runners had the flu, then the self-talk should be altered to reflect reality.

What if children fail? Then we must help them discover what they could have done better, learn from their failures, and work to improve their performances.

The practice of attributing failures to oneself regardless of the facts is untruthful. It is also untruthful to excuse all failures by attributing them to external causes when in fact they resulted from poor preparation, failure to practice, lack of effort, or unwillingness to cope with difficulty.

Working to develop competence is often better than introspection and always better than self-scourging.

Giving God the Glory

Does truthful attribution discourage the Christian practice of giving God the glory? Certainly not! The believer knows that there is no worthwhile competence or positive achievement that does not come from God. We couldn't activate a brain cell or move a muscle without His blessing. Any success we earn must be attributed to God's blessing and gracious gifts, but we contribute to the success through careful preparation which, though blessed by God, was nevertheless our preparation. If our attributional style prevents us from seeing the connection between success and *our own hard work*, we may simply "let God do it" when He has called *us* to do it. While salvation is the doing of God alone, we do have a responsibility to carry out His will. We need Him and His blessing to accomplish anything worthwhile in the kingdom, but He works through us.

Changing Attributional Styles

When untruthful attributional styles become truthful, changes will occur in children. A child who has been seen by others as a blaming, boastful, self-centered pain in the neck will become more socially accepted by other kids as well as by adults. A child who has suffered the agony of self-loathing and self-debasing will become more self-accepting, happy, and free. After all, Jesus' own promise that "the truth will set you free" applies as much to a child as it does to anyone else.

To help children change, we should first examine our own spoken attributions. This may not be as easy as it sounds. A truthful friend can sometimes help. Do we come up with attributions without giving it much thought, attributing causes stereotypically, according to a regular pattern? Do we always or usually attribute our own or our children's failures to such things as ill-fortune, bad neighbors, incompetent teachers, uncaring friends, demons, or even God—never to our own blundering? Do we always or usually attribute our successes or those of our children to circumstances, getting the breaks—never to skill, competence, or effort? Do we habitually attribute successes to the greatness or goodness of ourselves or our children? Are failures always because of personal badness, incompetence, or stupidity?

We must look for the styles, habits, and attributions we make without thinking. If we make attributions routinely, we need to learn to stop and consider the actual causes, because the truth is that some successes will be due to circumstances, but most will be due to skill, competence, and hard work. The truth is that some failures will be due to other people's malevolence or carelessness and other outside influences, but most will be due to our own blundering.

If we find our own spoken attributions are untruthful we should work to change. Unless we do, our children may learn untruth from our examples. We can try keeping a log of our attributions. At the end of every day, we can ask ourselves what successes we've had during that day and write them down, considering what contributed to these positive events. We can list our attributions. We can do the same thing with setbacks and failures. After a few weeks of this we will be able to accurately assess our own attributional style. If it isn't truthful, we can begin immediately to break our habit by replacing false attributions with truthful ones. We should write them down for a time until we begin to incorporate the changes into our routine. Our children need our truthful example as a model.

Second, we must pay attention to children's attributions. We might want to log them. If our children regularly miss the truth, their attributions will lead to an untruthful self-esteem. If they make stereotypical attributions to explain their successes or failures, we may want to help them work on changes.

Third, we can help our children recognize the pain caused by untruthful attributions. Especially with smaller children, we should use stories to teach, like the following one:

A little boy named Joe loved to try things he hadn't tried before. Joe's mother had bought a new washing machine. "Look, Joe," she said happily, "this is Mommy's new washer. It will take the stains out of *anything!*" She knew Joe liked to get into things he shouldn't touch, so she added, "Joe, I don't want you to fool with the washer or even touch it."

Joe thought, "I wonder if it will take the black out of this shoe polish." So he poured a whole bottle of his dad's best black polish into his mother's washer and turned it on. Then he reached into the washer and pulled out a towel to see what had happened. It was black. He threw the towel on the floor and pulled out some more things. Black! Everything in sight was smeared with black waxy stains. What a mess! The washer was black. The clothes were black. Joe was black.

Joe's mother was furious. "Why did you do that, Joe?" she demanded.

"You said it would wash out *anything,*" Joe replied, blaming his mother instead of admitting that he had done something he shouldn't have.

Whenever Joe did something wrong or made a mistake, he would say, "I couldn't help it; someone (or something) else made me do it." This habit of Joe's made his mother and father feel pretty bad. They realized they needed to help Joe learn to take responsibility for his own actions.

After telling this somewhat humorous story, you can ask your children what Joe's parents could have done to teach Joe to be more responsible.

Stories that illustrate children's habitual and untruthful attributions can quickly open up a discussion between parents and children and lead to changes in children's behavior.

Older children might relate to a more direct approach. Keep a log of the child's attributional statements for a while and then begin a conversation like the following:

Esther, I want to talk with you about something.

I've been listening to some of the things you've said over the past few days (or weeks) because I was interested in how you explained your successes as well as your mistakes and failures. I'd like to discuss it with you some night this week.

The goal of this process is not to make accusations or pin guilt on our children. It's to help them understand that their attributions are false and to show them the detrimental results.

This is the fourth principle. Not only must we examine our own attributions, pay attention to our children's, and help them recognize their false attributions, but we also need to help children state attributions truthfully. Here are some examples. In the first column are untruthful attributions; in the second, truthful ones.

False Attributions	Truthful Attributions
"I lost the game, sure, because Rob cheated."	"I lost the game because I didn't play as well as Rob. I need more practice." (Note how this boy sticks to a specific reason for losing—he doesn't write himself off.)
"My teacher seems to like me a lot, but it must be because she doesn't know me very well yet. When she knows me better, I bet she won't like me."	"I'm glad my teacher likes me. I'm going to work hard and try to live up to her high opinion of me."
"My paper wasn't very good, that's why I got an A− instead of an A. I'm not very good at writing papers."	"I got an A− instead of an A because I forgot to include a quotation from President Lincoln's Second Inaugural Address. I'll try to remember to include quotations next time." (She attributes her A− to a specific behavioral failure not her personal inferiority.)

False Attributions	Truthful Attributions
"I didn't get any complaints from customers on my paper route last month! They're probably saving them up for this month."	"I didn't get any complaints last month. It really helped that I worked harder than ever to make sure all my customers were well served."
"I'm not going to jump rope anymore. Everybody else does better than I do. I'm just no good at stuff like that. I quit."	"I haven't practiced enough with the jump rope. I'm going to practice more so I can keep up with the others."

Helping children change a faulty attributional style to a truthful one will lead to freedom from

- painfully inaccurate low self-esteem
- hopelessness and unwillingness to try
- pride
- being disliked by others
- incompetence and over-inflated self-esteem

Truthful self-talk stimulates positive and accurate emotional responses to successes and failures, which in turn contributes to healthy self-esteem as children learn to accept credit or blame, whichever is appropriate, without becoming either big-headed or down-in-the-mouth. When children learn to accept that life is a series of successes and failures, they can live above both. Neither great success nor great failure can destroy a person with healthy self-esteem.

5

The Power of Emotions

Getting in Touch with Truthful Feelings

"Feelings are *everything!*" one woman told us. "The purpose of life is *feeling good*, so emotions are all that matter." Sentiments like these aren't hard to find. On the other hand, however, some parents give the impression to their children that emotions have *no* place at all. Which is right? "Feelings are everything" or "Feelings don't matter"? Or are both views mistaken? Honest emotional awareness goes hand in hand with truthful self-esteem. We want to teach our children to recognize and embrace truthful emotions.

Accepting Emotion

The Bible provides examples of people who accepted their own deep, sometimes dark, feelings but who learned to balance them with tenderness and compassion toward others. The authors of the Psalms, for instance, made no effort to bury their feelings, even negative ones. Nearly every Psalm expresses the emotions of someone afflicted and frightened, angry and vengeful, or rejoicing and glad. The Word never orders the downcast soul to "snap out of it," but repeatedly shows understanding of the troubled heart.

53

God reveals that even He is an emotional Being. He rejoices over His people. Before the flood, He regretted that He had made man. God's terrible anger railed against the evil one.

Jesus endured the emotional turmoil of being an innocent man who knew He was about to be nailed to a cross. "My soul is grieved to the point of death," He confided to His three closest friends. Then He prayed fervently to escape the agony. Mark observed that Jesus was "distressed and troubled" (Mark 14:33). If while imagining these scenes we can remember that Jesus was God in human flesh, it should help us accept our own painful emotions as part of life. Many influential Christian thinkers have recognized the significant function of emotions. Augustine, who wrote early in the fifth century, left us a fascinating discussion of the place of feelings in the Christian life. He refused to condemn them, calling them "perturbations of the soul, which appear as right affections in the life of the pious."[1]

There is nothing improper, unchristian, or sinful about having strong feelings, even when they are negative.

Discerning what your feelings are and expressing them appropriately is the first phase in the development of truthful self-esteem. We judge ourselves by our feelings, and then, in circular fashion, we produce feelings because of our self-judgments.

"I feel so tense around other people! I must be a real dud," sixteen-year-old Greg reasons. And his thoughts make his tension even worse. Self-esteem is altered by emotions because of what we believe our feelings mean.

To have good, truthful self-esteem, children need to accept themselves as feeling persons. They must become aware of their own feelings and the feelings of others. And they must learn that feelings come from thoughts, but that thoughts don't necessarily come from reality. Feeling bad doesn't mean we *are* bad.

Learning to Label

Recently psychologists have been paying greater attention to the role of emotion in children. They are discovering strategies to help youngsters change maladaptive feelings. One such strategy is to teach children to label their feelings. When children know themselves well enough to accurately label what they are feeling, they have the advantage of knowing how others feel too. This is invaluable in the development of good communication and loving behavior. But before we get too far ahead of ourselves, let's learn how to teach children to identify their emotions.

Although it is important to teach our kids to understand their feelings, it is equally important to balance self-knowledge with lessons on compassion and empathy for others. We need to admonish ourselves, when necessary, to lighten up and keep the lessons enjoyable. We don't want to complicate the problem by making our young ones morose, self-centered, and introspective.

It is never too early to begin teaching little ones to name and manage their feelings. Of course, the younger they are, the more concrete their thinking will be. Very young children can only point to pictures to show they understand what they are feeling.

What Am I Feeling? A Learning Game for Preschoolers

You can begin teaching your preschoolers to tell themselves the truth about feelings with a simple game called *What Am I Feeling?*

Show pictures of faces displaying various emotions. (You may want to use the drawings in the Appendix.) Let children guess the emotion or name the feeling expressed on each face. For young children, start with simple feelings. For very young children, distinctions between *bad* and *good* or *happy* and *sad* might be enough. Later they can learn to discriminate between such things as anger, sadness, happiness, and fear. As the child progresses, try finer distinctions, such as that between disgust and anger or between happiness and peace. As the distinctions become finer, make allowances for imprecision. If you have puppets available, use them to act out various emotions for children to label.

This game can be repeated often before boredom sets in. You can vary the activity, letting children display feelings by play-acting with the puppets. Still another way for preschoolers to learn is by teaching friends or other family members what they have discovered. When they do the teaching, they learn even more. Adult supervision is still necessary, however, because the children will need clarification of some feelings.

Because preschoolers have short attention spans, keep the lessons short. If they are really into the game, use your best judgment to determine how long to keep it going. If you see signs of tiring, move to another activity. Keep things moving to prevent weariness with learning. It is best to stop the game *before* children lose interest.

We recommend keeping a diary of your child's achievements as you work through this book. It will be rewarding to see how much he or she has learned. Moreover, the diary will be a permanent record of what you have completed and what remains to be done. Perhaps one day it will be a treasured keepsake.

For First Graders: "Once upon a time. . . ."

The adjustments required of children entering first grade are enormous. They enter school expecting something like kindergarten: lots of fun, naps, half days, and play with other kids. For some, the unexpected reality may be so shocking and disruptive that it results in depression. Not only have the school days doubled in length, but demands and frustrations have increased as well. In addition, children may for the first time experience teasing, aggression, and cruel treatment by peers who also are learning to cope in a new and seemingly unfriendly environment.

Although parents generally know when their children are troubled about something, they may find it nearly impossible to induce the troubled child to talk about the problem. On such occasions, the game "Once upon a time. . . ." provides a context in which children can open up about their difficulties.

Some kids will understand this exercise immediately; others won't catch on without a demonstration. By demonstrating to your children how to express emotions, you validate their feelings and tell them it is all right to have negative feelings, but that it's important to know how to express them appropriately.

This game enables parents to detect misbeliefs in their children and to help their children replace misbeliefs with the truth. The following exchange is between six-year-old Debbie and her grandmother, whom she calls "Nana," on their way home after a day of shopping:

NANA: Let's make up some stories, Debbie. Let's play Once Upon a Time . . .

DEBBIE: Okay! You start, Nana.

NANA: Once upon a time . . .

DEBBIE: A little girl was very sad . . .

NANA: Because . . .

DEBBIE: She didn't know what to do.

NANA: She was puzzled and felt bad because. . . .

DEBBIE: Her friend was mean.

NANA: She was mean because . . .

DEBBIE: Because her friend had a birthday party and didn't invite her.

NANA: And so . . .

DEBBIE: She was sad because her friend invited their other friends and left her out.

NANA: But though the little girl was very sad, she always knew . . .

DEBBIE: That her Nana loves her very much.

NANA: And that . . .

DEBBIE: She will be having her own birthday party soon and she can invite whoever she wants.

NANA: And there is someone else who will never stop loving and caring for her no matter what happens . . .

DEBBIE: JESUS! The end! Let's do another story, Nana!

NANA: Okay! Once upon a time . . .

DEBBIE: There was an old lady—a granny named Nana!

NANA: She was so old . . .
DEBBIE: She had wrinkles all over her whole body!
NANA: And the grandma . . .
DEBBIE: Loved her adorable granddaughter Debbie so, so
          much!
NANA: And Nana . . .
DEBBIE: *Told* her granddaughter she was very adorable!
          The end!

There are several things to note about this interaction between Nana and Debbie:

1. The grandmother knew her little granddaughter must be feeling sad about something.
2. Nana didn't know where the story would lead, but ventured into it anyway.
3. The setting was casual.
4. Debbie and Nana seemed to have a close and loving relationship.
5. The little girl was saddened at being left out by her friend.
6. The grandmother validated the child's feelings, then directed the story to some known truths: (a) the grandmother's love; (b) the fact that there will be other parties so this incident isn't the end of the world; and (c) the unfailing love of Jesus.
7. The child was allowed to end the story when she tired of being introspective. To keep things light, she teased her grandmother.

Emotional Clues From the Body

By age eight, most children know there is a relationship between their emotions and certain things they feel happening in their bodies. They are able to understand that their bodies give them clues about their feelings.

You can elaborate on this by explaining that internal feelings, like butterflies in the stomach, tell us when we're scared, and that tense muscles tell us when we're angry. Use some examples that are common around your household. For instance, does Dad have a certain facial expression before he hollers? Does Mom change her posture when someone misbehaves? Does big brother clench his teeth just before he clobbers little sister? Does little sister get stiff if the neighbor's German shepherd comes around while she's playing outdoors?

Discuss what it means when muscles tense up, skin puckers up into goose bumps, or the heart beats faster. Explain that these physical reactions are often the first indication of the emotion a person is feeling.

Emotional education programs are now available to help youngsters get in touch with their emotions. Dr. Kevin D. Stark uses the following strategies with good results in his own emotional education program.[2] These games are excellent ways for kids to get in touch with their emotions. We suggest they be played in a family setting.

Games for Getting in Touch With Truthful Feelings

Emotional Vocabulary 1. Following is a list of common emotions. You can lengthen the list if you are working with older children or adolescents. You may want to shorten it to use with children younger than age ten. Write the label for each feeling on a 3 × 5 card. Shuffle the cards and let players take turns picking cards with the labels concealed. After selecting a card, the player reads the name of the emotion aloud and returns the card to the deck. Then the player describes the emotion, how it feels, and what was happening the last time he or she experienced that particular feeling. The child reaches the goal of the game by adequately describing each feeling in the deck. Hearing children describe these feelings and associated experiences is always interesting and often delightful.

Here is the list used by Dr. Stark:

happy	proud	upset
mad	hurt	guilty
sad	furious	left out
scared	jealous	put down
surprised	nervous	discouraged
lonely	ashamed	relieved
bored	excited	confused

Emotional Vocabulary 2. In this game, children practice explaining the relationships between thoughts and feelings and between feelings and actions. Use the "feeling cards" constructed for the previous game. Players take turns picking cards at random without seeing the words on them. The child reads the name of the emotion aloud and then describes how a person experiencing that feeling would be thinking and acting.

Use this game as an opportunity to teach about the intensities of emotional experience. Help children differentiate between mild, medium, and strong when they describe the various feelings.

Emotion Charades. A player draws a card at random and reads it *silently.* He or she thinks for a moment about how someone feeling that emotion would look and act. Then the child acts out the emotion without making a sound or saying any words. The others try to guess the emotion being acted out. Players take turns drawing a card and acting.

A variation might be to have two teams. The first player for team A draws a card and displays the emotion as instructed above. The other players on team A try to guess the emotion within a certain time limit, say, one minute. If they come up with the correct label within that time, they get a point. Then it's team B's turn. The winning team is the one with the highest score after all the cards have been used.

Emotion Statues. One player will be the sculptor, another the statue, and the others will be the audience. The sculptor chooses a card at random and reads the label silently. After taking a moment to think, he or she shapes the statue's facial expression, posture, arms, hands, feet, and legs in such a way as to show the feeling. Then two more players become sculptor and statue. This continues until everyone has had a turn playing each role.

Emotional Noises. Each player takes a turn drawing a card, reading it silently, and then expressing the emotion solely by sounds (i.e., by using noises, not words). The others try to guess the correct label for the feeling being expressed.[3]

Sentence Completion. Sentence completion can be used with preschool through grade-school children. Say the first part of a statement and let the child complete it. When complete, the sentences make an emotional statement.

Examples:

- I like it when . . .
- I don't like it when . . .
- The best feeling in the whole world is . . .
- The worst feeling in the whole world is . . .
- One thing I like about my mom/dad/brother/sister is . . .
- One thing I dislike about my mom/dad/brother/sister is . . .
- I like it when my family . . .
- I don't like it when my family . . .
- Today was a good day because . . .
- Today was a bad day because . . .

Adolescents

Some of the above activities can be adapted for older children and adolescents, but adolescents generally prefer a less structured, more casual setting. Try to get them talking when you're taking a walk, playing games, cooking or baking, shopping, riding in the car, working, or doing some other project.

Because of the notorious unpredictability of most teens, be ready to talk whenever the opportune moment arises. You can't predict when teenagers will have a volatile day and will need to tell someone how they feel. Be available!

Every so often they may even have a good day and let you know about it!

Always be alert for opportunities to help your youngsters get in touch with their feelings; it is the first step in teaching them to live competently—with truthful self-esteem.

The woman who said "Feelings are everything" had things out of perspective. Feelings are not everything, but they are clues to everything. How we and our children feel about the things going on around us is perhaps the most important clue we have as to what we are saying to ourselves and whether or not it is truthful. We cannot ignore emotions and hope to raise healthy children. Neither, however, can we depend on our emotions to tell us the truth.

6

Managing Strong Feelings

Helping a Child Who Feels Overwhelmed

Amanda felt overwhelming sadness when her grand-mother died. There were special things she had wanted to tell her, but now she would never get the chance. Like Amanda, many children have emotions they don't know how to manage because they haven't learned how to express their feelings appropriately. So they may perpetuate their feelings with misbeliefs for years, even into adulthood.

Is there a better way for children to handle their emotions? Can we help them find truthful expression for their feelings?

What Is a Truthful Emotion?

A truthful emotion is a feeling, good or bad, which is brought into subjection to God's will. When the feeling is anguish, it will be like that of Jesus when He was praying, "Not my will but Thine be done." If it's anger, it will be righteous and measured like the anger of God. If it's joy, it will well up at the good fortunes of others, not only when things go well for ourselves. Such emotion flows naturally from truthful self-talk.

Appropriate emotions must be based on believing and telling ourselves the truth. What we call "untruthful emotion" occurs in response to inner talk or beliefs that contain lies. Untruthful emotions for children may be momentary anger at not getting their way, anxiety over brief separation from a parent, or long-lasting gloom after a friend moves away. Such feelings result from untruthful beliefs and self-talk.

Feelings and Facts Are Not the Same

Some adults have never learned to distance themselves from their feelings. They haven't learned that feelings are not reality. Nor have they noticed that certain related thoughts pop into their minds whenever they feel particular emotions. It is even more difficult for most children and many adolescents to distance themselves from their feelings. Children in particular seldom notice the links between their feelings and their self-talk. They think of their feelings as caused either by nothing or by external events. In fact, they often take their emotions as proof of the conditions outside themselves. But the truth is, changing emotions do not reflect the way reality is! Nothing could be more to the point than this lesson.

Our Thoughts About Life Make a Difference

If emotions don't reliably reflect reality, what do they reflect? Our emotions faithfully show our *interpretations* of reality. Emotions demonstrate our thoughts about life and the meanings we choose to invest in events.

If I choose to interpret the loss of something as an indication that God doesn't love me, my emotions will reflect hopelessness and discouragement. For if God doesn't love me, I have very little reason to hope that things will turn out well for me. Eventually my life will crumble into nothingness. When I allow such interpretations to run through my mind unchecked, they will cause me to feel sad, dispirited, hopeless, small, and discouraged.

If I choose to think that a friend's careless oversight means that she doesn't really care about me, my emotions will trail along behind these thoughts and reflect my anger. If I think similarly about most of my relationships, I will have few abiding friendships indeed.

If I choose to make a string of financial reversals mean that I am a real loser, destined to always come out as the tail and not the head, my feelings about myself will reflect my self-disgust.

Feelings Reflect Thoughts

When we show our children the connections between their thoughts and their emotions, we give them a potent tool for controlling distressing, destructive feelings. We show them that they can decide what kind of thought diet their minds will feed on, that they can be victors, not victims, that they can control their feelings rather than be controlled by them. They will learn that the source of their sadness or badness or anger or dissatisfaction is their thoughts, and that thoughts can be changed. When we teach them how, we will have given them a key to liberty.[1]

The Thought Detective

Dr. Kevin Stark has suggested a brilliant technique for teaching youngsters to get in touch with their thought life: the thought detective, *Mr. Searchbrain.*[2] Mr. Searchbrain can help him collect evidence for maladaptive thoughts. He can help detect feelings, too. Try something like this:

I want you to met Mr. Searchbrain, the thought detective. We will pretend he is in your head right now. You can get him to help you find out what you're feeling and why you're feeling it. And most important, he can help you decide if you're feeling a truthful emotion or an untruthful one. Then he can help you to change it if you want to.

Detectives look for clues, don't they? Well, when you ask Mr. Searchbrain to help you discover what you're feeling, he'll ask you if you have any clues. "What is your first clue?" Mr. Searchbrain asks.

As the child pretends he's feeling an emotion, show him how to imagine Mr. Searchbrain is asking about his thoughts, his bodily reactions, his facial expression, his posture, his impulses, and what he feels like doing.

What is the evidence? Or, what is your first clue? In the case of *anger*, the detective can help the child identify what various levels of anger would be like, from neutral to intense rage. After he labels his feelings, he thinks about the bodily sensations that accompany each label. Anger usually progresses in stages. It is very important for a child to notice the progressive stages, and then to very clearly identify the feelings that accompany them. Ask him when he first knows he's getting angry, and how does he know?

MR. SEARCHBRAIN: Would you like to have my help so you can find out what's making you feel upset?

CHILD: Uh-huh. I guess so. It's just the way my dad is, that's all.

MR. SEARCHBRAIN: Your dad upset you?

CHILD: Yeah. He ate all the Cap'n Crunch.

MR. SEARCHBRAIN: You wanted some Cap'n Crunch for yourself?

CHILD: It's the only cereal I like. I can't stand the other stuff. I'm not gonna eat anything!

MR. SEARCHBRAIN: So we want to find out more about why you're upset. Any clues in the pit of your stomach?

CHILD: My stomach feels all knotted up inside.

MR. SEARCHBRAIN: Pretty tense, huh? How about your shoulders?

CHILD: They feel tight. And my face feels hot. Is my face red?

MR. SEARCHBRAIN: I think so. Any other clues?

CHILD: I feel like when Jerry took my first baseman's mitt last week. I wanted

	to hit somebody and that's the way I feel now.
MR. SEARCHBRAIN:	Sounds to me like you're mad. Whom would you like to hit?
CHILD:	Well, I couldn't hit my dad, but he's the one who upset me.
MR. SEARCHBRAIN:	You're mad at your father.
CHILD:	Yeah. He ate my cereal, and now there's none for me. I don't want any other kind either, so don't tell me to eat the other stuff. I'm not gonna eat.
MR. SEARCHBRAIN:	Okay, but wouldn't you like to feel a little better—wouldn't you like to get over feeling so upset and tense?
CHILD:	Well, it's my dad's fault. He made me feel this way.
MR. SEARCHBRAIN:	You said you'd like my help. Want to feel better?
CHILD:	I guess I do. How are you going to help? There isn't any more Cap'n Crunch. And that makes me feel bad.
MR. SEARCHBRAIN:	You can't feel better by telling yourself it's all your dad's fault, and you can't feel better by thinking you have to have a bowl of Cap'n Crunch before you can get over this. You have to look at what you're thinking because your thoughts are making you upset.
CHILD:	No they aren't. It's my dad.
MR. SEARCHBRAIN:	Aren't you telling yourself your dad treated you badly?
CHILD:	Sure. He did. He didn't think about me and what I want. He only thought about himself. That's what he always does. He only cares about himself and he doesn't care about me. He made me upset!
MR. SEARCHBRAIN:	Anything else about your dad?

CHILD: He should think about other people before he takes all the stuff they like!

MR. SEARCHBRAIN: So you're telling yourself it's your father who upset you, and that he did it by eating all the cereal you wanted without stopping to think about you and about what you want. You're saying your dad doesn't care about you—doesn't love you or pay any attention to what you want. Sounds like your father is a pretty bad guy.

CHILD: Yeah—(pause) well, I don't think he's always so bad. Sometimes he isn't. Sometimes he does things I like. I like it when he plays ball with me or reads to me or brings me stuff.

MR. SEARCHBRAIN: You think maybe you don't want to tell yourself that your father was bad and that he deliberately upset you and didn't care at all about you when he ate the cereal you wanted?

CHILD: He might not have known we didn't have any more. Or maybe he didn't know I wanted Cap'n Crunch this morning. Maybe he didn't mean to do it. Maybe he just didn't know.

MR. SEARCHBRAIN: You're thinking your father may not have meant to hurt your feelings or take the cereal you wanted? And are you also thinking he would have shared with you if he'd known you wanted Cap'n Crunch and that there wasn't another box in the house?

CHILD: Yup, that's right. I'm telling myself those things. I guess I might want some of that other cereal after all.

MR. SEARCHBRAIN: So you feel better? Less upset? It helps to tell yourself that your dad didn't mean to hurt you or ignore

	you? It feels better when you remind yourself of how often he plays with you and tries to make you happy? So the whole cereal problem was just an accident and not something your father did because he's mean?
CHILD:	I guess so. I feel a lot better. What you just said is what helps. And it's the truth too.
MR. SEARCHBRAIN:	Can you see how your thoughts about things can upset you and make you angry, and how changing your thoughts can sometimes make you less angry and upset?
CHILD:	Yeah, I can. This cereal isn't so bad either. I'll have another helping.

Mr. Searchbrain can help children reveal their thoughts and help them understand how their bodily reactions, facial expressions, posture, and impulses are signs of how they feel on the inside. It is the body that first gives clues about what children are feeling. When youngsters learn to recognize their bodily sensations, they will maintain better control of their feelings. Once they begin to understand their feelings, Mr. Searchbrain can uncover untruthful thoughts. Then he can teach them how to manage their feelings and tell themselves the truth.

Using Charts

School-age and adolescent youngsters may find the use of charts helpful. The *Strong Negative Feeling Management Worksheet* in the Appendix will help children track their persistent negative thoughts and behaviors. You can use rewards to reinforce their efforts to change their feelings.[3] Reward children first on the basis of daily ratings and then later move to weekly totals.

How long should charts and reinforcement be used? Obviously, we don't want to have to give our children money, treats, and privileges forever. We want them to cope with their negative feelings effectively. And we want them to do it because they appreciate the improvement in their own peace of mind, not solely for the things they earn.

Tangible reinforcers should be gradually discontinued in any child training program as the desired behavior becomes habitual. Wait until the target behavior becomes nearly second nature; then begin to give tangible rewards less frequently—and preferably unpredictably. So, instead of offering a tangible reward every time points are totaled up, do so occasionally and at random.

Little by little reduce the frequency of tangible rewards until they fade out of the picture. Do not, however, stop giving genuine, loving approval. The most important rewards a parent can give are social reinforcers. A warm smile, an approving tone of voice, a pleased demeanor, and an expression of praise can't be surpassed as reinforcement.

Changed Thoughts?

Can we change anger to happiness, grief to contentment?

Remember Amanda, who was sad because her grandmother died before she'd had a chance to tell her some important things? Amanda's mother suggested that Amanda write her grandmother a note even though her grandmother had already died. Amanda followed her mother's advice and wrote about how sad she was and how much she missed her. She even expressed her anger about some things. She knew no one would ever see what she wrote, so she was free to write the truth. "I miss you so much, but I know you are happy in heaven with Jesus." Carefully, unobserved by anyone, she slipped her note under the pillow in Grandma's casket. Almost immediately, the heaviness lifted and she felt a smile coming to her lips. Amanda detected her feelings and dealt truthfully with them. And it helped her deal with self-talk and emotions that could have hardened into abiding misbeliefs, possibly to wreak havoc later.

Helping children learn to release feelings involves teaching them to change their thoughts, and changed thoughts come from a changed will. What children need to discover is their will.

Earlier psychologists (like the great William James) and nearly all Christian thinkers have taught that we *can* use our wills to manage our feelings. Hannah Whitall Smith, author of *The Christian's Secret of a Happy Life*, explains the crucial distinction between centering life in the emotions and centering life in the will. Although her book is often considered a devotional classic, it is also a valuable psychological self-help manual on feelings and will, as the following reveals:

> Now, the truth is that this life is not to be lived in the emotions at all, but in the will; and therefore if only the will is kept steadfastly abiding in its center, God's will, *the varying states of emotion do not in the least disturb or affect the reality of the life* . . . It is sometimes thought that the emotions are the governing power in our nature. But I think all of us know, as a matter of practical experience, that there is something within us, behind our emotions and behind our wishes, an independent self, that after all, decides everything and controls everything. Our emotions belong to us, and are suffered and enjoyed by us, but they are not ourselves; and if God is to take possession of us, it must be into the central will or personality that He enters. If, then, He is reigning there by the power of His Spirit, all the rest of our nature must come under His sway; and as the will is, so is the man (italics added).[4]

So our children can learn not to depend on their feelings to tell them the truth about reality. They can learn to use their wills to replace misery-creating self-talk with truth. That is why we must not neglect our children's emotions *or* their wills.

7

When Your Child Is Depressed

Lifting Spirits With Truth

Parents know how their children feel—don't they? Not necessarily. Some youngsters can put up a front, wear a mask over their feelings. A facade of carefree nonchalance may disguise feelings of depression. ("I don't care if I don't have anyone to play with—I'd rather throw the frisbee for Spot anyhow!") Other unwanted feelings may lie buried under a flurry of activity. Even irritability can cloak something else—unhappiness or sorrow perhaps. Let's consider how you can tell when your youngster is feeling sad and what you can do to help the child feel normal again.

James

"Hey, James, let's talk about our camping and fishing trip on the Klamath River. You know what's waiting for us there? Steelhead!"

Neil Isaacson couldn't believe his son's response, which amounted to a shrug and a sigh. "Okay, Dad. What do we have to talk about? (Sigh.)"

73

Neil tried again. "You've never hooked into one of those babies, Son. Just wait. They break the surface, they dive to the bottom, they run you up and down the riverbank. They do everything but grab the pole and hook *you!* What a thrill!" Neil was lost in old memories—how his dad had taught him to catch his first steelhead. He got an adrenalin rush just thinking about it.

"Yeah." James's half-hearted acquiescence brought Neil thudding back to the here and now. What was wrong with the boy anyway? Ever since midway into seventh grade he had changed. Where was the happy, energetic, ready-to-try-anything kid who had taken over the family camping trips and added zest to any shared activity?

Later, Neil and his wife, Julie, shared their bewilderment. "He doesn't care about fishing for steelhead or anything else. I can't figure it out!" Neil said.

"He hasn't been himself lately, that's for sure," Julie agreed. "He's so grouchy he bites your head off for nothing. He sulks; he's restless; he won't cooperate unless you force him to. I don't know what to do."

"And what's happened to his grades? They've gone way down! Maybe it's just growing pains. I don't know what else could be wrong," said Neil, shaking his head. Both hoped the trip would snap their son out of whatever was wrong.

Pamela

"I don't get it, Doctor," said Pamela's mother to the school psychologist. She had asked for an appointment to discuss her concerns. Her nine-year-old had changed—radically—in just the past few weeks. "She has always been the 'strong-willed child' Dobson's book describes! Then a couple of months ago she suddenly got quiet. She is actually compliant and sweet as pie! But she doesn't seem to want to do anything at all! This passive child is *not* my daughter! She even does what we tell her to do without arguing. It's wonderful, but it's not *her!* Something's wrong."

Not many parents would come in complaining about a

child turned compliant, thought the doctor. *But I'm glad this mother is here. I think there is a problem.*

Patrick

"What's going on with Patrick?" the teacher asked Patrick's father. Patrick had always been a little aggressive, but now things were out of hand. "Last week he beat up Lance, his best friend," said Mrs. Halvorson, "and today he even tried to beat me up!" This kindergarten teacher had never before faced an overt attack by a five-year-old.

Patrick's father later supplied some sad details about their crumbling family. Later, Patrick himself offered significant information.

Kids Don't Tell, They Act Out

You can ask your child what is bothering him/her. Most often, you won't get a satisfactory answer because children, unlike some adults, don't typically interpret, clarify, and explain their problems and how they feel about them. Instead, they show their difficulties in their behavior. They "act out." When your child changes behavior radically, something may be radically wrong. It's the child's way of saying, "I feel bad and I don't know how to talk about it." Sometimes it's hard, even for adults, to put into words what the problem is. Yet it's easier for adults to process things and eventually verbalize what's troubling them. Young children find it much more difficult.

One of the duties of parents is to help children learn to articulate what's wrong and deal with life's troubles. Observing and interpreting what we see is part of our job. Instead of dismissing puzzling changes in the child's behavior, take it as an alert. Find out what the problem is. Your child might be depressed. You probably can help.

Detecting Depression/Sadness

Can children become depressed? Absolutely. When parents see no indication of sadness on a child's face, the possibility might not occur to them. After all, isn't childhood a happy, carefree time? What could cause depression in a kid with nothing to worry about except what game to play next? Unfortunately, depression and sadness are no respecters of age!

What you see when a child is depressed may not be what you see in a depressed adult. A very young child might be glued to his mother. He clings to her, objecting strenuously if she leaves his side. He balks at going to Sunday school or daycare. Older kids might become restless, crabby, and aggressive—or oppositional and contrary, refusing cooperation, opting out of family activities. An older child might avoid other kids and withdraw to her room where she spends most of her time. This child might stop paying attention to her appearance. Other signs of sad, hopeless, discouraged feelings: A child complains about difficulties at school; she talks of leaving home; she says nobody understands her and nobody gives her approval. Maybe she's more emotional and more sensitive, getting her feelings hurt and interpreting the actions of others as rejection. Because children may not tell you straight out that they feel bad, you have to figure it out. Look for out-of-character expressions, sadness, sleep difficulties (either insomnia or sleeping too much), and appetite disturbances (either not eating enough or overeating). He has lost interest in things he used to like. He gets no pleasure out of his favorite activities. Nothing is as much fun as it used to be. He appears to lack energy.

What You Can Do About It

What can parents do? Most parents, upon noticing some peculiar change in their sons or daughters will ask, "What's wrong, honey?" The odds are your child will answer, "Nothing," or, "I don't know." For many reasons, children usually can't tell you what the problem is. Instead, they act out, showing you by their conduct and manner that something is awry. It's not that they want to cause difficulty, it's just hard to put into words what's bothering them, particularly if their feelings are new and strange. Parents, here is what you must do: *Observe, listen, talk, empathize.*

Observe! Listen! Find the precipitant. The first thing to do is very practical. Ask yourself what has changed in the circumstances of the child. Nearly all depression is brought on by a change that has great significance for the individual. Remember, look for changes that matter to the child, even if they have little importance to you. Has the child been ill? Did someone significant move away or die? Has she lost a pet? Might a close friend have moved away? What has happened at school that the child might consider a major loss? Did she fail at something she considers essential? Has the household changed? Is there a new family member? Was there a separation or divorce? Has someone been treating her badly, picking on her, rejecting her, threatening her? Each of these situations involves perceived *loss* of something meaningful.

When psychologists think a person may be depressed, they look for a precipitating event that the individual might construe as a loss. If your child appears depressed, consider what may have precipitated the problem. By getting a handle on the originating factor or event, you may learn a great deal about what can be changed to bring about recovery. Think back to the three vignettes at the beginning of this chapter. When James's parents asked themselves what had happened that James might perceive as a major loss, they were thunderstruck. Of course! A month ago, Garth, his best friend since kindergarten, moved to a distant city. For several years, James had depended on Garth for companionship. The boys were always together. Closer than brothers, they had never thought about life without each other. James saw the move as a major calamity. It was enough to precipitate an episode of depression.

Discovering the precipitating event for Pamela's depression involved a little more observing and listening. The psychologist asked her to draw things that made her sad. The nine-year-old surprised him by picturing a courtroom, a judge, and a man and woman glaring at each other. Obviously, the man and woman were getting a divorce. Pamela stopped after finishing the drawing. It was enough. With it, her mother's thinking was stimulated to recall that divorce had reared its ugly head in Pamela's life. The divorce of her best friend's parents occurred just before the onset of Pamela's depression. Was she thinking that she, too, could lose her home by a tragic divorce? With this clue, Pamela's mother and father could help their daughter express her fears openly and to give her helpful and truthful reassurance.

What about Patrick's aggression? His loss wasn't hard to pin down. His mother had suddenly moved out of the home, abandoning Patrick and his sister to the care of their father. Patrick had no trouble verbalizing his loss: "I want to beat people up because I'm mad," said the five-year-old. "I'm mad because my mom left us and we need her. She says she won't be coming back!"

Listen, observe, and think. Find the event or events your child has understood as a major loss. It might also help to talk to others who know your child.

Talk with the child. The way you talk makes a difference. It's easy for the depressed child to hear the voice of an adult authority as threatening or badgering. "What's wrong?" may sound to him like, "What in the world is wrong with you, anyhow? Shape up!" "Why are you so quiet?" can seem to be a demand for change. The way you come across may suggest to the depressed child that you are complaining about her behavior or that you find her unhappiness aggravating. She may think you're telling her she should try harder to meet your expectations. Remember, a depressed child is already down on herself. She believes she's worthless, helpless, useless, or reprehensible. So try not to offer glib advice she can't handle like, "Cheer up. You'll get over it," or, "Now, now, you know God will take care of you and you shouldn't be discouraged. Just take it to the Lord in prayer," or, "Snap out of it."

Show empathy, understanding, and acceptance of negative feelings and the reasons for his depressed conduct. Let him know you understand that he feels miserable. Here are some examples of empathic statements. Remember also that showing empathy involves appropriate expression, not words alone:

- "It must be awfully painful to feel like you've lost the friend you need most and won't ever get him back!"
- "No wonder you don't feel like doing much. I guess it's pretty hard even to get out of bed in the morning."
- "It all looks fairly hopeless, huh?"
- "Does it seem hard to figure out how things can get better?"
- "It's not much fun to have Mom leave, is it? I feel bad, too."
- "I imagine you feel quite hurt."

Get the child to express his thoughts about the situation. "What do you think [the loss] means? What makes it so awful?" Try to help the child explain the meaning of the event to you. You may find that she interprets events so inaccurately you wouldn't have thought it possible! She might be attributing the loss to her own defects. Does she believe someone's leaving proves she is not loveable? Is she telling herself she is incapable of coping without the person she has lost? Is she convinced that the loss has ruined her life? Has she convinced herself things will never improve? Self-talk like that is typical of depressed people.

One word has been used to characterize the thoughts of depressed people: *devaluation.* In depression, children, like adults, devalue everything. Specifically, depression involves devaluation in three life domains: self, circumstances, and the future.

1. Self-devaluation. Depressed youngsters believe they are incompetent, inadequate, or worthless. The emphasis may vary. One child may explain his losses by reasoning that he isn't attractive or good: "I know Mom wouldn't have left us if I'd been a better kid." Another may reason in the opposite direction, contending that the loss is so devastating he's rendered useless or helpless: "I won't be able to make it without him. I'm just no good on my own." One tells herself she is incompetent. Another dwells on personal unattractiveness or even ugliness. The idea that nobody loves her because she's not loveable may plague her. Or else she may tell herself, "I can't do anything right." The stress may be on personal worthlessness, incompetence, deficiency, or unattractiveness.

2. *Devaluation of circumstances.* What are the signs that a child devalues his circumstances or his daily life? He may simply appear listless, bored, and uninterested in anything. Prospects that once would have brought a sparkle to his eye he now greets with a heavy sigh. When Dad suggests a fishing trip, he has all he can do to acquiesce. When Mom invites him to a cookie feed, he reacts without enthusiasm. He thinks, "It won't be any fun," or "I don't know what to do," or "I don't want to." Such responses may be accompanied by restlessness, inability to stick with anything, and complaints that there isn't anything to do. Depressed kids tell themselves that their circumstances are aversive and that life is not worth living.

3. *Devaluation of the future.* To a normal, secure child, the future appears bright and full of promise. Wonders lie ahead when Christmas or Easter is just around the corner. The coming summer vacation holds untold delights, and she can't wait for school to get out. But when she is depressed, the future looms ahead, holding nothing but pain. She can't imagine getting through the school year or the next week or even today. She would rather not think about it. She tells herself that her losses are permanent. She believes her personal inadequacies and her painful existence won't improve. The future is bleak and hopeless. Listen for expressions suggesting hopelessness and discouragement. They may be clues to depressive self-talk that downgrades the child's future.

Correct devaluative self-talk. Your task is to help the child correct devaluative self-talk. Why? Because it is untruthful and because it generates and perpetuates depression. Notice we have never said that the child's sadness and depression were *caused* by loss. The loss only triggers or precipitates depression. It is the child's untruthful beliefs and self-talk that maintain and worsen his sad, hopeless mood.

When he discovers the truth and alters his self-talk accordingly, his mood will improve. He can learn that he is not worthless or incompetent or friendless, but valuable, lovable, and capable of worthwhile accomplishments. When he stops believing the false notion that there is nothing interesting or pleasurable left in life, he will have good emotions again. When he sees that the future is far from hopeless, he will tell himself the truth. He will understand that when he gets out and tries fishing for steelhead or making cookies or making new friends, the effort will be worthwhile. The experience will be rewarding even though it may not appear so now. When he grasps this truth, he will begin to feel better.

You can help your child discover and tell himself the truth. Don't put him down as you help him correct his misbeliefs. After you have listened with empathy, let him know what you have heard him say: that he is telling himself depressing and discouraging assertions. Repeat his depressive self-talk for him. Get him to notice how he really is thinking and believing what you have verbalized. Then help him to see how devaluative beliefs can make a person feel bad—like he feels. Ask him to imagine how different he might feel if he told himself truthful and positive things. Show him the falsehoods in his depressive self-talk, and help him to create truthful self-statements to replace them. Practice the new self-talk with him. Your exchange with him might go something like this:

"Sounds to me like you're telling yourself you'll never have a good friend again."

"Yeah, well, I don't think I'll ever have a friend like Eric. We've been buddies ever since we were in fourth grade together."

"Uh-huh. I can see why you'd think nobody will ever replace him. And I guess in one sense, nobody will. Every friend has special qualities. Once you've really become buddies it's hard to give him up. Did you ever think about the fact that you might visit Eric or invite him to visit you?"

"I've thought about it. But I don't believe that would satisfy me. I still wouldn't have a friend when I got back."

"Couldn't you work on making friends with somebody else?"

"I've tried. But all I think about is that it's not Eric. And I'll never really enjoy anyone as much. I don't even want to go to school now that he's gone."

"You mean you'll never be happy again without Eric? Is that what you think?"

"Yeah, I think that's true, Dad."

"Tell me something. Was there a time in your life when you and Eric weren't friends?"

"Well, sure. I met him when we moved here—in fourth grade."

"Were you ever happy before fourth grade?"

"Of course. That's a silly question! I had a great time at my old school before we moved."

"You were happy before you ever knew Eric?"

"I see what you're getting at. Hmm. I was happy before I knew Eric, so I guess it isn't so terrible having to get along without him again. I *can* make a new friend, can't I?"

"Do you think you could work on not telling yourself you're worthless without Eric? Could you maybe force yourself to think a little more truthfully about your life?"

"Maybe I could. Thanks, Dad. I feel a little better."

Look for self-talk in which the child has been overlooking the fact of God's love and God's providence. Much depressive self-talk has come originally from the Devil who devises devaluative thinking to make us despair. If he can make us disregard God's love and God's resources, or make us deny our worth in God, he can generate despair. Help your child get his self-talk on a track that incorporates the mighty truths he has learned in Sunday school!

Get the child activated. If you can persuade him/her to do things, so much the better. Depressed children may become inactive, refusing to play or work, sitting in front of the television, or just doing nothing. They tell themselves that all activities are unrewarding or even aversive. The fact is that when they actually get involved in an activity, very often it turns out to be more rewarding for them than they thought it would.

What Not to Do

Don't ignore depression. Don't make the mistake of ignoring a hurting child or adolescent. The consequences of unrecognized depressive thinking can be grave. If you teach yourself to replace his devaluative thoughts with the truth, you will give him something he can use throughout his life. He will be equipped to prevent relapsing into depression later.

Don't tease. Occasionally, we may make the mistake of trying to tease a child to bring her out of her down moods. Don't. Good-natured teasing may have its place when both parties are in the spirit of the thing and everybody is feeling playful. Teasing is seldom in place when a person is hurting. You may discover that you have cut off any avenue of communication if you persist in teasing a child who is in despair.

Don't overreact. Another mistake is to push the panic button. Threatening to take the child to a psychologist if she doesn't stop moping may seem an efficient way to snap her out of it, but it won't work. It will only widen the gulf she already senses between her and you. It may increase her despair.

Don't say, "When I was your age . . ." Talking down to him, a preemptory tone of voice, telling him how your mother forced you to snap out of it, or otherwise pressuring the child to act as though he isn't depressed will only deepen his feelings of loneliness and convince him that you don't understand. Stay focused on the child and on his feelings and thoughts.

Should You See a Specialist?

What if you have tried your best to help, but the child shows no improvement? You might want to consult a Christian psychiatrist or psychologist for advice. Your doctor or your pastor can probably refer you. Be sure to ask first if the person you consult has specialized in treating children. If not, has the expert had much experience in recognizing and treating children's disorders? Some counselors, very effective with adults, have no expertise in treating youngsters. Once you have located a knowledgeable person whose values are similar to yours, you would do well to follow that person's advice.

8

Practical Help With a Child's Anxiety

Confronting Those Unfounded Fears

"Friends, childhood is such a carefree time of life! How we envy our little ones their sun-filled days of play and long nights of deep, untroubled sleep 'while visions of sugar plums dance through their heads!' " The speaker warmed to his subject as the spellbound audience nodded unthinking agreement. Not so! It is a myth that children enjoy lives free from fear and anxiety. The notion that childhood is a snug, secure time, unruffled by any threat, is fantasy.

If you take the trouble to look at real children and listen to them carefully, you will find that normal youngsters endure occasional anxiety. Anxiety is fear, but fear that is pointless, needless, and based on untruthful beliefs. When a child is afraid of a situation presenting no real threat, we call such fear *anxiety*. Worry is a kind of anxiety. Normal children sometimes worry. And, like adults, they usually worry about eventualities that will never occur.

Do Normal Children Suffer Anxiety?

Parents often have to cope with their children's fears, anxieties, even terrors. Many normal children suffer from fear of the dark. Many develop fear of deep water, or of getting their faces submerged in water. Some kids shy away from strangers, certain animals, loud noises, new situations, and the unknown. Others hate and fear being alone. After her very first plane trip, seven-year-old Corrie adamantly refused another one. "No, Grandma," she explained, "I'm not afraid of flying on the plane, only of crashing!"

Seven-year-old Jamie worried because sometimes she didn't *feel* love for the people she *said* she loved. Did she really love them? She didn't know, so she asked what Mother thought. Jamie's mother said she too sometimes couldn't feel the love she knew she had for others. Jamie felt better when her mother told her everybody has ups and downs in their feelings.

Andrew, age nine, felt tense and nervous—with hyperactive butterflies in his stomach—whenever kids chose up sides for a game. He might not be chosen until last, and that would mean he was no good, he thought.

Many young children are like little Twila, afraid of separation from their mothers, worrying that they will be abandoned or forgotten. She resisted starting kindergarten because of her anxiety.

The Big One: Fear of Losing Mother and Father

Children get anxious about physical harm and death, abandonment, rejection, pain, injections, new situations, and disapproval, among other imagined threats. But the most common childhood worry is *separation anxiety.*The child becomes upset when he is taken out of his accustomed environment or away from people to whom he is attached. His anxiety may accelerate to the point of panic. He cries, he screams, he may even gag or vomit. Terror reigns, and reassurance doesn't help much. This reaction comes from the facts and conditions of childhood. The human infant is thoroughly dependent on others from the moment of birth through several years of life. He is not only emotionally attached to his care-givers; without them he will die. They are his link to survival. If the idea enters his head that he may lose them, it is for him the threat of extinction, even if he doesn't think it all through to that conclusion.

"I don't know what's wrong with Gail," Five-year-old's worried mother informed her father. "I couldn't convince her to go to school today. She wouldn't get on the bus. I gave up when she got so upset and I couldn't calm her down. I decided to let her stay home."

"I don't get it," muttered Gail's father. "I thought kindergarten was supposed to be fun. How come she doesn't like it?"

"It is fun! She has a marvelous teacher and the program is excellent. I don't know what the problem is. Maybe she'll feel altogether different in a day or two. I don't think we should push her."

But Gail didn't feel different the next day. Or the day after that. In fact, the more her parents tried to cope with her anxiety by letting her stay at home, the tighter she clung to her mother. Gail was developing a serious case of separation anxiety. Like the parents of many children with separation anxiety, Gail's mother and father were a close-knit couple who gave their daughter much love and care. They talked together about Gail's fears without coming to a workable solution. But they kept asking questions and reading books.

Robert's parents and their friends thought of him as the perfect eleven-year-old. He strove to please his parents, his teachers, and his friends, and had almost no quarrels with others. He was careful to do the right thing at all times. But Robert did not see himself as successful in relationships. "Nobody cares about me," he would tell himself. "I wish I had never been born." Why? Tune in on his secret fear and preoccupation with it. Robert couldn't shake off a feeling of dread that an awful illness or fatal accident would befall him or his parents. When Robert's friend Mark invited him to his house for supper and to sleep overnight, Robert refused. Persuasion didn't change his mind. Robert simply couldn't bring himself to stay anywhere overnight unless his parents were with him.

Her mother's friends did not enjoy visiting her mother because Joanne, age nine, made their visits miserable. She never let go of her mother's attention, but demanded constant interaction even when Mother tried to chat with a friend. For Mother, there wasn't a chance. Joanne repeatedly interrupted her, demanding service: "Mom, could you try to find my jump rope right now? I don't know where it is." Joanne's stomach hurt whenever her mother left her with a baby-sitter.

Bill didn't like to be away from home. And because he was fifteen and a varsity athlete, he hated his fears. Ever since he could remember, he became nauseated when he stayed with baby-sitters. There had been some years when his fears subsided, but others when they got worse. Lately, even thinking of staying away overnight gave him other, more frightening feelings; heart palpitations, dizziness, feelings of faintness. When the family physician performed a detailed examination, he found no organic disorder. The doctor felt sure Bill's problem was anxiety, so he asked about his fears. But Bill—like most older boys with this problem—denied being especially concerned about his mother. He was ashamed to admit to being the "Momma's boy" he considered himself.

Four-year-old Walter's headaches mystified the pediatrician until he asked Walter's mother to keep a detailed record. Then it became clear that Walter regularly developed a headache a day or two before visiting his father who lived in another city.

Let's look again at Gail. Gail's parents read about ways of dealing with her anxiety. One day they forced her to go to school. She cried and threw herself on the floor. But they were desperate. They had tried every kind of persuasion to no avail. At last, they made up their minds to force her to stay in school. Her father took her to her classroom, put her in her seat, and told the teacher to keep her there no matter what. Soon after he left the school, Gail vomited. Like many other victims of what might be called *school phobia*, she became panicky when she had to be separated from her mother. This anxiety we call *separation anxiety* tends to occur in kids who come from close, loving families.

What Anxious Children Believe

Though we can't quote Gail's self-talk for you, no doubt she believed and told herself what other children with similar fears tell themselves. Here are some of the thoughts from the internal monologues of children with *separation anxiety* (or *school phobia*):

- "Something dreadful will surely happen to me. I won't be able to handle it without my mother (or father) to help me. That will be so terrible I may not live through it. I might even die. My parents are my only link to life. They'll probably die. I'll never get over it."
- "What if my mother goes away and I don't have her anymore? What if she gets sick? If I don't keep her nearby, she might be kidnapped or killed. Then what would happen to me? I couldn't survive!"
- "My daddy left me because he and my mom couldn't get along. How do I know my mom won't leave me, too? She's the only one I have left, so I'd better keep my eye on her."
- "I don't know why, I just want to be home. I know I haven't been gone more than a few hours, but I don't feel right unless I'm in my own place. I think a lot about how good it will feel to see Mom and Dad when I get home. I can't wait!"
- "If I don't keep my mother's attention all the time, she might overlook me and even leave me. So I should keep interrupting to make sure she doesn't forget me."
- "How can I hang on to to people I desperately need? I'll try to be perfect, get their attention, and keep their love. If I don't, I might lose them."

How Did He Get So Anxious?

"Ross has always been fearful and easily upset," explained his mother. Why? His brother, Les, hasn't given us a bit of trouble. He's never been afraid of *anything!*" The boy's mother was exasperated when Ross refused to try new experiences or to venture far from the familiar, safe haven of home. She often asked herself why.

Her husband thought the answer was to be found in their son's past. "I think Ross must have had a terrifying experience when he was a baby. It's the only explanation. I guess we'll never know what happened to him."

The truth is that Ross and Leslie were born with different genes. Even though they were brothers, each had a different *anxiety threshold*. They were constitutionally different people. If you build a doorway, you can make the threshold as high or low as you choose. If you make it very low, only a small person can cross it. If you make it very high, a taller person can come over the threshold into the room without difficulty. Picture the threshold in the doorway between your child and fear. If his threshold is low, he has a low tolerance to fear. Les had a relatively high threshold, so fear and anxiety were not a problem to him. People with low thresholds like Ross become more easily upset. Sometimes we call this low emotional threshold a "short fuse."

Unreasonable Fears: Loss, Criticism, and Harm

Besides the fear of separation, children and adolescents make themselves nervous, fearful, worried, and anxious about three other common notions: *loss, criticism, and harm.*

Fear of Loss:

- "I'll probably lose my best friend one way or another. I always do." (Loss of a significant other.)
- "If I enter the contest, I'll most likely come out near last—I can't win."

- "I know I won't do very well on this test. It will pull down my grades." (Loss of approval, admiration, respect due to poor performance.)
- "They all think I'm a great hitter, but I'm afraid I can't keep it up and they'll find out I'm just average." (Loss of approval, admiration, and acceptance due to failure to perform.)

Fear of Criticism:

- "What will people say about me if they find out my dad is an alcoholic?"
- "I can't let people know I'm not a good reader or they might make fun of me."
- "I can't go to school. My dad won't let me wear my hair like the other kids. They'll think I'm a nerd!"
- "I'd better have a beer with them or they'll say I'm chicken."
- "I'd like to say *Fröliche Weinacht!* to Mr. Schulz—wish him a Merry Christmas in his own language, but I'm afraid people would think I'm showing off my German."

Fear of Harm:

- "I might get hurt if I play football."
- "All strangers are dangerous. They will hurt me."
- "If I walk to school alone, the big kids might beat me up."
- "What if the horse throws me off?"

Self-talk Generates Anxiety

To help yourself and your child with anxiety, begin by grasping the fundamental premise that people make themselves anxious. At first, you may not want to buy that notion. "No way," you respond, "I don't make myself anxious. All I have to do is take an elevator to the top of a skyscraper and I turn to a bowlful of jelly. It's the distance between me and the ground that does me in."

And, of course, you are right—except for one thing you

might be forgetting. *You have to* know *you are at the top of the tall building before you can get anxious!* "So what?" you answer. "Of course I have to know how high I am before I get anxious, but how can I help knowing when I ride an elevator for ten minutes to get up there?"

Still, if you have to *know* you're up high before you get anxious, it's not your location that makes you anxious. *It's what you tell yourself about your location!* What if someone blindfolded you and took you for a simulated elevator ride. Wouldn't you be uncomfortable if you *believed* you were fifty-seven stories above the earth even though you were on solid ground all the time? Of course you would. Now do you see how your *belief* and not your *location* causes your distress? And if you truly believed, while fifty-seven stories high, that you were as safe as if you were home in bed, you wouldn't get upset, would you?

"I guess you've got a point," you say, "but I can't help believing I'm in terrible danger when I'm up there. Down here, reading this book, I can see how my fear is faulty and my belief that heights are dangerous is silly. But when I actually get to the top of a building, my beliefs change and I *can't stop believing I'm going to fall off!*"

Now we agree. Your beliefs are what turn you to jelly, but so far you haven't been able to control your beliefs very well when you get into your own anxiety-generating situation. The same is true for your anxious child.

Nearly everyone's anxieties are generated by similar misbeliefs. True, the particular threats are different for different people, but the form of anxiety-arousing self-talk, for you and for children, involves telling oneself:

Proposition #1: Criticism, or loss, or harm, or heights, or horses, or deep water, or flying, or failure, or being alone, or _____ (fill in the thing your child fears) will very probably happen to me if I'm not extremely careful to prevent it.

Proposition #2: If _____ happens to me, that will be

unendurable, catastrophic, dreadful, beyond what I can tolerate.

Proposition #3: I am now or am about to be involved in a situation where I won't be able to prevent _____ , so it might very well happen.

If a person rehearses this set of propositions to himself, they will generate the unpleasant and frightening physiological response we call anxiety. Depending on the age of the youngster and other factors, he will notice excessive sweating, palpitations, tense muscles, tremors, jittery weakness, light-headedness, or other signs of nervous arousal. So most people—most children as well as adults— try to control their lives so that #3 won't ever be the case— that is, so that they never expose themselves to the dangers propositions #1 and #2 threaten.

How to Counter Anxiety

Several years ago, some psychologists began asking themselves what would happen if people challenged proposition #3 by exposing themselves to situations where they become anxious. Would they get worse or better? Certain facts about behavior discovered in experiments on animal anxiety demonstrated that the natural tendency to *avoid* such situations caused anxiety to remain strong and even become stronger. However, those who went ahead and faced their fears instead of avoiding them found their anxiety to diminish. Forcing themselves to enter harmless but feared situations and remain there, they eventually stopped believing that danger threatened and that they would be harmed or destroyed. Of course they changed their belief because *experience forced them to face facts!*

The following is a set of simple instructions for working with your child to counter anxiety:

1. Make a plan laying out practical steps for encountering and handling the threat. Rehearse it frequently.

"If there is a fire in our house, here is what we will do

first . . . then . . . and . . . finally . . ."

"If you are assigned a talk to give before the class, here is what you can do to prepare and give your speech: Outline it, write it, read it over, practice delivering it alone, practice delivering it with an audience, practice with a larger audience, give your speech in class."

"If your friend moves away, you may feel some sadness. This is what you can do to make up for the loss of an important person . . ."

Molly, age fifteen, became tired of the burden of her own separation anxiety. She decided to face down her anxiety rather than let it overwhelm her. She told herself: If you spend the night at Suzie's house and you begin to think about what might happen to Mom in your absence, you will tell yourself the truth: "The chance of anything bad happening to Mom is so low it's not worth worrying about. Even if she should get sick or injured in some way, Dad will be there; he will call 911, the paramedics will come and she'll be just fine. And even if I do worry a little or feel a little anxious at first, the important thing is that I'm actually staying away from home for a night and that's my goal. I don't have to feel perfect about it."

2. Don't force your child to confront the source of his fears. Help him to simply try the things he fears and investigate the unknown in nonthreatening ways.

NOT: "Where did you ever learn to be so afraid of monsters? What on earth makes you think there's a crocodile under your bed? What makes you such a coward?"

BUT: Lead the child gently into testing the fear for himself. Put your own head under the bed first. Say, "See, my head wasn't chopped off. Now you put one hand under the bed. Good. Anything happen? Want to try a whole arm? Good. Now how about both of us putting our heads under and having a look. Great! Now how do you feel about it? Ready for me to turn off the light so you can sleep?"

3. Encourage the child to talk with you about fears and anxieties.

4. Take one step at a time toward the goal of doing the frightening thing. Don't try to conquer the problem all at once.

5. Take the child's fears seriously. Don't ridicule. Don't act censorious or put the child down for having fears, no matter how trivial or foolish they may seem to you. Your fears probably seem trivial to God, too. But He doesn't put you down. He helps you. You take the same stance with your child.

6. Be an example of calm! Get your own anxieties under control and make your own self-talk truthful. If you scream when there is a thunderstorm, what do you expect your child to think and do?

7. Monitor TV, books, and magazines. They can be sources of fear and threat.

8. Don't confuse natural hesitation or normal caution with fear. Let the child approach new things at his own pace.

9. Teach the child to look at the self-talk and beliefs that cause anxiety and seek to change them. Don't try to psychoanalyze him to "get at the root of the problem."

NOT: "What has made you so fearful and dependent on your mother? How did you get this way? Can you think of anything in the past that made you think you'd lose her?"

BUT: "Why not see whether what you're telling yourself is correct? Is it true that if you go to school your mother won't be here when you get home? What makes you think that? What is more likely? If, for any reason, you came home and your mother wasn't there, where would she probably be? If she's not at home, and you don't know where she is, does that mean you'd lose her? Never see her again? Why not tell yourself the truth and see if you feel better about going to school? You will be going to school today and if these ideas come into your head, plan to counter them with the truth."

10. Praise small achievements when your child overcomes anxiety-arousing situations.

Facing the Anxiety in Imagination

Sometimes an anxiety-arousing situation can be faced gradually in the imagination. You can help your child do this best when she is relaxed rather than tense and fearful. Choose a good time together and, with the child's consent, do the following:

1. Have the child sit in a comfortable position or even lie down. Say, "Now just close your eyes, relax, and take a deep breath. Imagine the air going clear down to the bottoms of your feet. Hold it. Let it out slowly." Do this three times.

2. Tell the child, "God says He will never leave you. Can you picture His big strong arms? Can you imagine Him holding you safe and sound in those strong arms? Let yourself feel safe and secure there. Let yourself believe His promise to take care of you no matter what."

3. "Tell me how it feels right now to know God is close and is taking perfect care of you." Let the child tell you, his eyes closed, what the picture is like.

4. "Now picture your mother leaving for one minute. God is still holding you. Mother will be right back. How did that feel? Now picture Mother leaving for two minutes." Continue to lengthen intervals. With other fears, adapt this model as needed to present the feared object or situation in gradually increased doses mixed with vital faith that risks everything on God's care and love. If the child becomes anxious, stop and induce calm before going ahead. Back up and repeat earlier scenes if necessary.

5. "If you feel scared, it's all right. You can fight your fear with the Word of God and His promises. Tell yourself the truth about God's love, His care, His closeness, and His protection."

6. "Tell yourself you can feel real achievement when you overcome the fear even for a little while."

Make these sessions frequent and short—no more than twenty minutes to half an hour—shorter for younger children. Combine them with plans for the child to begin experiencing small doses of the feared situation.

A Final Note

One last word to parents about anxiety: You naturally want to comfort your fearful child. But watch that your comforting doesn't turn into unintentional reinforcement for the child's fears. You can strengthen those fears by inadvertently rewarding the child for having them. Here are some ways parents might unintentionally reward a child for being anxious:

- Routinely staying with the child when he says he is afraid, canceling your plans and ignoring other obligations.
- Allowing him to sleep with you when he says he wants to because he is afraid.
- Letting him stay home from school because of anxiety. A common device for children who are anxious to avoid something is to complain of physical symptoms ("My stomach hurts." "My head aches." "I feel sick."). Be "wise as serpents" and do not permit yourself to be duped into reinforcing anxiety by abetting avoidance.
- Allowing a child to avoid important events simply because the child says she is afraid (going to the dentist, physical education classes, swimming lessons, social activities, for example).
- Giving the child reason to believe that the best way to deal with fear is to avoid the thing feared.

Gentle encouragement to try things and take them in small doses while telling himself the truth is the best medicine you can give your anxious child.

9

"You Make Me Angry!"

Exposing the Lies That Lead to Rage

A few days before we wrote this chapter, a youngster at school took a gun out of his pocket and shot another boy who had insulted him. A few weeks earlier, a driver on a Los Angeles freeway pulled alongside another car and shot the driver. Presumably the victim had done something to irritate the gunman. Do your children watch the eight thousand murders a year presented to them on television? In the unreal world of the tube, anger is cool and murder is a reasonable response to insult. So why are some people still mystified by high rates of aggression in society? Angry feelings destroy marriages, damage children, ruin friendships, and complicate relationships with misunderstandings. Much anger goes unrecognized because people act it out in passive, indirect ways. Resistance, stubbornness, and just getting things all messed up may be nothing more than angry behavior in disguise.

Some misguided parents smile indulgently at their children's aggressive conduct. They tell themselves that aggression is good because no other children dare to pick on their son or daughter. That may be true, but unless the conduct changes, these children will hit snags in social relationships, or worse, wind up in serious trouble with the law. Because they intimidate others, others may defer to them, but angry, aggressive children will never be well-liked.

Do parents with aggressive children have anything to be concerned about? Yes, definitely. Research has shown that aggression in young children foreshadows aggression and delinquency in adolescence. And it doesn't go away by itself. Unless something happens to change things, children who show aggressive habits early in life will continue in the same pattern. Anger and rage in childhood is something all parents should take seriously.

Recognizing Anger and Aggression

Anger and aggression are not identical terms, but they are related. Unrestrained emotional explosions, violence, hitting, breaking things in rage, and getting even are examples of aggressive actions. Anger, however, sometimes wears a quieter face. For example, the "silent burn," during which children avoid talking to show they are mad, is an example of anger. Some anger is so hidden and indirect it is all but unrecognizable. Children who tease animals or pinch babies when no adult is looking may very well be angry.

The difference between aggression and anger is that anger is an *emotion*, while aggression is the *behavior* that results from the emotion of anger. Anger is feeling. Aggression is action. People feel anger when they have been hurt or when they see injustice. Most of us learn to curb our aggressive impulses most of the time. When children pout, they are angry. When children react to a command by screaming, they're showing anger. When they hit a younger sibling, they are showing aggression.

When we describe youngsters as "angry," we are not referring to those who get angry only occasionally. We mean those who respond to many situations with anger, those for whom anger is a pervasive mood. We also mean those who use aggressive behavior to handle problems. Angry youngsters lack self-control. They are impulsive. They act before taking time to weigh the consequences of their actions. So they may do things that get them into trouble more often than others do.

An episode of anger has four stages: (1) An event is perceived as a provocation. (2) The event is interpreted within the child's internal monologue as being unfair and having great personal consequence. (3) The child's self-talk prompts physiological stimulation: The nervous system responds, muscles become tense, the heart rate speeds up, blood pressure increases, perspiration begins, and blood flow to tensed muscles increases. All these events prepare the child for action. The child feels anger. (4) The child acts overtly. Aggressive behavior occurs at this point unless something interrupts the process. Even so, some action (even if it is only stubborn resistance or a peeved facial expression) usually shows the child's anger. These four elements aré what we mean when we speak of getting angry.

Focus on Self-talk

Parents have very little, if any, control over stages one and three of the anger process. Parents cannot alter the environment enough so that children never experience provocation (stage 1). Nobody can get through life without being hurt and treated unjustly. Nor can parents do much about the inflamed phase (stage 3) because children are wired to respond automatically to their beliefs and self-talk.

So what can parents hope to change? What can they work on with anger-prone children? Parents can and should train their children to stop after stage 3 and weigh the consequences of the overt behavior they are considering (stage 4). Aggressive behavior that seems justified during a fit of anger will be seen as self-defeating when children can learn to stop and think, think, think, even though their body is telling them to act, act, act.

What is better, however, is to help children change their beliefs and interpretations concerning the provocation—

that is, change their self-talk (stage 2)—so that is where we will focus our attention.

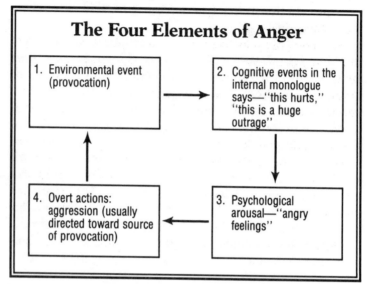

The Four Elements of Anger

1. Environmental event (provocation)

2. Cognitive events in the internal monologue says—"this hurts," "this is a huge outrage"

4. Overt actions: aggression (usually directed toward source of provocation)

3. Psychological arousal—"angry feelings"

By changing beliefs and self-talk, children can decrease their angry feelings. By substituting truth for illogical, anger-arousing assumptions and inward utterances, they can prevent themselves from becoming infuriated and upset over events. Moreover, they can gain control over their impulsive, aggressive actions.

It Doesn't *Seem* to Be Cognitive

Marge objected when we mentioned that her twelve-year-old son's outbursts of rage might have something to do with what was going on in his mind. She wasn't impressed with our suggestion that cognitions generated her son Tony's fury.

"You're telling me that he actually thinks before he starts screaming at me and hitting me?"

Tony's responses seemed too emotional and volatile to stem from any kind of thought process. Marge would rather have been told her son had nitroglycerine in his blood. She just didn't see how he could be instigating his own outbursts by what he told himself.

"His reaction doesn't look like it involves thought to me," Marge insisted.

Her response was like that of other people we've talked to about anger—even adult clients who are trying to get help to control their own anger. The trouble is that the explosion occurs so fast that it seems spontaneous. There doesn't seem to be time for self-talk before the big bang.

But there is time. Thoughts can flash through our minds so fast we don't even notice them, much less identify them. A whole set of beliefs, moral judgments, expectations, attributions, self-statements, and problem-solving tactics lurk in our subconscious, exerting their power *even when we have no awareness of them!*

The following are the kinds of beliefs angry people habitually rehearse in their internal monologues. On the basis of these beliefs their emotions carry them away:

- "People should treat me in certain ways, and when they don't, I have to get upset so they'll know I deserve better treatment."
- "When events don't occur in the way I expect, I have to show my disapproval to keep things from going wrong again."
- "My way is best, and I have a right to have things done my way. If they're not, I have to show anger so that people will do things my way the next time."
- "People do things I don't like because everyone is against me."
- "She hurt me intentionally."
- "The best way to solve some problems is to get angry (or act aggressively) because then others will do what I want."
- "When others neglect my wants and needs, they don't care about me, so I have to do something to show I am important."
- "When anything goes wrong it's someone else's fault, and it's important for me to find out who is to blame

and to show irritation at the one who caused the trouble so everyone will know I had nothing to do with it."
- "Other people should always think of me first."
- "Things should always go my way."
- "People should always notice me and respect my wants and feelings."
- "Events set me off. Circumstances cause me to get upset. Other people make me mad."
- "If I don't talk to her, she'll realize she's done something wrong and ask me about it. Then I can tell her how much she hurt me and that will make her feel bad. Then we'll be even."
- "If I make him wait for me, he'll realize how I feel when he makes me wait and that will make him change."
- "People [or events] make me so upset I can't control myself—I just can't."

New Self-talk for Angry Kids

Angry children need to learn new interpretations, replacing their false, negatively biased interpretations with self-talk statements that generate forgiveness, love, and peace instead of anger and hostility. Here are the kinds of self-statements you can teach your children to dampen their anger and forestall aggression:

- "When events don't go my way, it doesn't mean everything in the world is bad."
- "There's no reason for me to get upset when people don't treat me the way I want them to. It's hardly awful!"
- "My rights haven't been violated every time I don't get my way, because God never said I have a right to get my way all the time!"
- "It's not the end of the world when others don't care about me as much as I'd like them to. People have a right to their preferences. I can handle it."
- "It's wrong to think other people will treat me better if I get even with them."
- "I *can* control my behavior."

- "I should get more information. There might be a reasonable explanation for my friend's hurtful behavior."
- "He probably didn't mean it. Maybe he was just trying to get my attention."
- "Is there anything else I should consider?"
- "They don't mean to criticize me. Maybe they just don't understand me."
- "He must have been joking. He probably didn't mean to put me down."
- "Other people don't have to care about me and notice me always. They have a right to think about something else instead of me."
- "Events and circumstances don't make me upset. I make myself upset."
- "Other people don't make me mad. I make myself mad."
- "Getting mad isn't the way to solve problems or make things better."

Missing Cognitions Make a Big Difference

We have seen how beliefs and self-talk lead to angry outbursts. But the problem comes not only from what is *there*. What is *not* there can also cause trouble! What is *missing* has a lot to do with impulsive actions, too. Perhaps you never noticed how you talk yourself *out* of morally wrong behavior. What gives you self-control and the power to reign in your strong feelings so they don't lead to rape, murder, and mayhem? Do you know? The fact is, your self-control comes from beliefs and self-talk.

Eugene Methvin, author of *The Riot Makers: The Technology of Social Demolition*, tells of a psychologist at the scene of Newark's 1967 riot. The psychologist saw a twelve-year-old boy watching looters with shopping carts empty a store. The boy stood by, shifting uneasily. The man put a hand on his shoulder. "What's the matter, son?" he asked.

"It's crazy. I don't see no sense in it!" the boy exploded.

The psychologist threw out a shrewd guess, naming a parochial school with strict moral training. "Do you go to St. _____ ?"

Wide-eyed, the boy replied, "Yes, sir. How did you know?"

The psychologist knew that the internal speech shaping that youngster's response to the chaos around him had been learned somewhere. Most likely, he thought, the boy had learned it at a religious school. His guess turned out to be right.

Methvin insists that civilization's first line of defense against savagery is family, church, and school—the institutions that inculcate morality.[1]

Moral principles are really cognitions that put the brakes on us when we feel an impulse to do wrong. This boy apparently believed in absolute right and wrong, so when he talked to himself he probably said things like, "Sure, you might feel like helping yourself to a TV set, but it's wrong to take other people's property."

When children fail to learn these and other cognitive brakes, the result is impulsive—often destructive—actions. Angry adolescents characteristically fail to tell themselves any self-control type statements.

That is why parents need to teach angry, aggressive children to tell themselves the truths that slam the psychological brakes on impulses to act unwisely or immorally. Here are some of the statements these kids need to practice telling themselves when they get upset. These and other similar self-talk sentences have been found to change angry and aggressive habits:

- "I don't have to get upset. God will help me. I can control my anger and figure out a better way to handle this situation."
- "I can calm down, take a few deep breaths; then I can figure out how to handle this situation."
- "Hold it. If I get kicked out of school, I can't graduate."
- "The Lord says it's wrong to hit people, so I'm going to control myself and talk to Len instead. I'm going to find out what he meant when he said those things about me."
- "I'd better stop and think about the consequences."
- "It's not right to lose my cool and I don't have to. I can

stop right here and relax, then I can use problem-solving skills to deal with this."
- "I'll try to stay cool and *listen* to their explanation. Some people really do care about me."

For children whose anger problem is combined with an uncontrolled temper, first train them to exercise self-control and then work on changing their beliefs about aggression and anger.

Family Role-Play to Cure Angry Aggression

When the problem is anger, impulsivity, and aggression, parents need to do more than simply tell children the truth and help them locate misbeliefs. Once anger has become a habit, children need to learn and practice new responses to angry feelings. One of the best tactics for teaching this is role-play. Have one person take the part of the provoking person, another can play the child's angry self-talk, and a third can be the child's new, self-controlling, forgiving self-talk.

To prepare for practice sessions, think of typical scenes from a child's daily life that depict provocation. Write these scenes on index cards and keep them available for future use. Here are some examples:

Tim enters the family room and sees his little brother playing with Tim's favorite road-racer set.

Sarah's big sister wants her to get out of the den so she can talk privately to her friend on the phone. She yells at Sarah and calls her a noisy, nosey nuisance.

Lisa wasn't saying a word, but her teacher bawls her out for talking to the girl next to her.

Come up with your own scenes from your own child's life.

Here is a sample role-play: Mom, Dad, and Johnny are working on John's habit of striking out in anger at whoever provokes him. Try doing it this way:

John has been playing marbles with a friend. The game is over and John's friend starts to collect his marbles. He picks up John's best aggie and puts it into his pocket. John says, "Hey, that's my aggie you just stuck in your pocket."

Dad will play John's friend, Mom will be John's old, angry self-talk, and John can act out his new, self-controlling self-talk. Ready?

DAD: (playing John's friend) No, it's not. It's mine. I've had it for a long time. Just ask my mom.

MOM: (playing John's old, angry self-talk) He's lying and he's trying to rip you off. You can't let him get away with that! Knock him down, take your marble, and tell him you'll never play with him again. That will teach him a lesson he'll never forget.

JOHN: (playing his new, self-controlling self-talk) Why should you get mad? It's just a marble. He's your friend. He's not trying to rip you off. He really thinks it's his. He *could* be right too. Stay cool and think about this. You can figure out how to solve this problem if you just stay calm and think.

Controlled by Anger No Longer

If you have felt hopeless about trying to help your angry child change, take heart! Many people have learned to control their angry feelings and impulses, and so can children. The difficulties created by uncontrolled behavior are enormous. It's worth whatever effort it takes to teach your offspring new self-talk and to give them the priceless gift of self-control.[2]

10

Self-Mastery

Developing Self-control With Self-talk

It's as normal for children to lack self-control as it is for puppies to wiggle or kittens to chase balls of yarn. No doubt you've met some of the following children:

Just before supper, when she is tired and hungry, Kathy gets grumpy, cries for no apparent reason, pesters her mother, or torments her little brother.

Maria knows she won't be hungry enough to eat her vegetables without an argument, but she sneaks a handful of M&Ms before dinner anyway.

Homework is nobody's favorite pastime, but for Danny it seems impossible. After every miserable report card discussion with his father, Danny tells himself he's going to do his assignments *every night*. It works for a few days, then something comes up and all his good intentions go down the drain.

When Melanie entered grade seven, she had to go from room to room for classes. She never seemed to have the proper books, pencils, pens, or notebooks for each class. Poor Melanie had never learned to think ahead and plan.

Twenty-five minutes precisely! Pastor Howard's sermons were always the same length. But Lance couldn't sit still and listen to them. He felt wiggly. Before long, he felt the urge to go to the bathroom. Sometimes he even punched his brother so his dad would take him out to the narthex.

Three-year-old Molly wants what she wants when she wants it and screams until she gets it.

Patti, thirteen, already has a reputation for being late. How long it will take to do her hair and press her blouse are mysteries she has never bothered to solve, so she doesn't allow time for them.

Carl would rather park himself in front of the TV than practice shooting baskets.

Self-control and Children

There is nothing very unusual about any of the above scenarios. They all involve youngsters who have not developed self-control in certain areas. Although the lack of self-control is natural, God wants His people to develop self-control. Good self-control and truthful self-esteem reinforce each other. If children learn to master their restless spirits, they have a reason for not tearing themselves down. If they have a good attitude about themselves, they will be able to practice godly self-control.

Good self-control generally involves proper behavior in two domains:

1. Resisting temptation
2. Planning for the future

Self-control Is Not an Impossible Dream

Can we teach children self-control? Can they develop this important trait while they are young? Yes, but self-control in children starts with parents. They have to be the model. If they are unable to control themselves, it's unlikely their children will have much self-control.

Self-control comes from learning to use the will. We have a will because we are made in God's image. God exercised His will in creation and also in salvation (James

1:18), and He gave each of us a will. Fleshly willpower is nothing but stubbornness, but when God himself works faith in us we have the power to exercise a new will. As the apostle Peter said, we can use that transformed will through God's Spirit and Word to partake of the divine nature. One of the results will be self-control (2 Peter 1:3–8).

Neither we nor our children will always succeed. But if we trust God to release our new Spirit-directed wills, He will do so. We can then learn the truths that lead to self-control and teach them to our children.

Learning Self-control by Talking to Ourselves

Psychologists have discovered that when people want to control themselves in a situation, they often talk to themselves, sometimes out loud. And some therapists have developed successful programs of self-talk to control temper outbursts. Of course, what you learn to do in such programs is to *change* the way you talk to yourself. People learn to control their temper by repeating such self-talk phrases as "Cool it, Mickey! You can keep calm. You can handle this without blowing your top. Stop and think. What would be the best thing for you to do right now instead of having a temper tantrum?" Christians know that the truthful self-talk of faith engendered by the Holy Spirit can offer mighty power over temptation *when they really use it.*

Learning Self-control in Temptation

Some psychologists recommend mentally altering a situation to make something forbidden less tempting. For example, they would have children say to themselves, "Those candies aren't really candies, they're just marbles," or "That TV show is probably just a rerun anyway, so I don't really want to see it."

Although this tactic might inhibit forbidden behavior, *it is not the truth* and we do not recommend it. Let's stick with the truth! "That candy sure looks good! But I know it's against the rules to eat it before dinner," or "That show is one I really like, but I need to do my homework now. I can always catch it when they rerun it," or "Stop! Think! What will the consequences be if I do it? If I don't?"

To train children to have self-control in tempting situations, begin by asking them the question: "What happens when people don't control themselves?" Follow that question with a story about a time you didn't exercise any self-control and describe the consequences. After the story, ask another question: "Can you think of a time when you should have controlled yourself and you didn't? What happened? How did you feel afterward?" This will get them thinking and talking about how critical self-control is. Continue the discussion with the story of Jesus' temptation:

> The Bible tells about a time when Jesus felt tempted to do wrong. Maybe you think Jesus could never feel the urge to do something sinful, but He did. God's Word says that He got the same feelings we get! But He never gave in to them. One day He started fasting, and He went without food for over a month—forty days! So He really felt starved. He was out in the desert where there was nothing but the scorching sun beating down on Him, barren rocks and sand, and a few scrubby plants. But there was absolutely nothing to eat. Now who showed up? The Devil! He knew just where to look for a weak spot in Jesus. "If you are really God's Son, why don't you just make these rocks turn into bread so you won't be hungry anymore?" Satan asked.
>
> And do you know what Jesus did? He talked back. He answered the Devil's evil suggestion with the truth: "Satan, the Bible says that a person doesn't live by physical food only, but by the truth of the Word of God." By believing and telling himself this truth, Jesus kept from doing what the Devil urged Him to do. Instead, he continued fasting, just as He was supposed to do. Two more times the Devil tried to lure Jesus into sin, but Jesus used the same tactics

every time. He told himself the truth right out of the Word of God! And every time it worked. He kept himself under control and He did not sin.

How did Jesus make himself tell the truth to himself? How did He bring himself to speak God's Word to himself rather han just repeat the thoughts generated by Satan? He used His will. He imitated His heavenly Parent just as your child will imitate his earthly parent, using your example as a model. Look at this:

"In the exercise of His will He brought us forth, by the word of truth, so that we might be, as it were, the first fruits of His creatures."[1]

As God exercised His will, and Jesus exercised His will to summon the truth to His aid, you can learn to demonstrate the use of the will for your children, and they can learn to exercise their wills to say truth to themselves instead of the tempting falsehoods that can rob them of self-control. You won't read much about *will* in psychology books. Most psychologists believe man's behavior is merely a result of the external forces exerted on it by heredity and environment. But God's Word has not omitted will.

You too can *will* to tell yourself the truth when you are tempted by Satan, your own desires, or another person! And so can your children. You can control yourself with the help and power of God, whose Word is truth.

To apply the truths from the temptation story, one family had the following conversation:

PARENT: Let's see if we can come up with some situations when we are tempted to do what we know we shouldn't do. I can start. Yesterday in the store, the clerk gave me too much change—a dollar more than I had coming. I remember thinking, "I could just keep this extra dollar and not say anything to anybody." But then I made myself think of what God's Word says, "Thou shalt not steal," and, "Do good to all men." So, in my self-talk, I said,

"No! I'm not going to keep the extra dollar. I'm going to give it back because I don't want to take what isn't mine, and I do want to do good to the clerk." Then I said to her, "Here. I think maybe I got an extra dollar with my change. Have a nice day." I don't always make myself think of the truth, so I don't always do things right, but that time I did. How about you? Can you think of a time you heard Satan telling you to do something you shouldn't?

JONATHAN: I can, Mom. I was mad at Muriel this morning when she took my school pencil and wouldn't give it back.

PARENT: What happened? Did you think anything in your mind that wasn't right?

JONATHAN: Yep! "Hit her! She's got it coming, the little snot!" That's what ran through my thoughts.

PARENT: Where do you think that suggestion came from?

JONATHAN: The devil—just like when he tried to get Jesus to turn stones into food.

PARENT: What did you do, Jonathan? How did you handle it?

JONATHAN: Well, I got ready to hit Muriel, and then I decided to ask myself what I should do. I think I used my will to tell myself, "I don't *have* to hit her. And it won't help. It'll just start a big fight. I should love my sister and not hurt her, even if she isn't doing right. What else can I do instead to solve the problem? I do need a pencil. I've got it! I'll get another pencil from Dad's desk. I know he won't mind." And that's what I did.

PARENT: How did you feel after that?

JONATHAN: Well, I was still a little mad at Muriel, and I don't think she ought to take things that are mine, but I feel good that I told myself the truth and didn't hit her as I have before.

Invite the rest of the family to come up with some more

situations in which they were tempted by misbeliefs. Encourage children to tell of some situations in which they might have failed to resist and actually did the wrong thing. Be sure to use these as an opportunity to teach them to self-talk the good news of forgiveness and restoration through Jesus.

MURIEL: I want to tell about a time when I *didn't* tell myself the truth. Angie and I were playing hopscotch Saturday morning. Rhonda came and wanted to play and I wouldn't let her. I should have been nice to her, but I wasn't.

PARENT: What were you telling yourself?

MURIEL: I guess I was thinking, "Rhonda's a nerd. I want Angie all to myself. Besides, if Rhonda starts playing, she'll beat me and I'll never get a turn. She always butts in! I wish she'd go away!"— stuff like that.

PARENT: Were those thoughts truthful?

MURIEL: Well, Rhonda does play better than me. And sometimes she and Angie go to her house and leave me all alone. But, no, she doesn't *always* butt in, and anyway, I could have asked her to play. If she and Angie left me alone, I could have gone to Sonja. She was home and I know she likes to play with me. So I guess my thoughts weren't very truthful. Specially when they made me treat Rhonda badly and hurt her feelings. Those thoughts weren't very loving, were they?

PARENT: No, they weren't. And I can see you feel bad about what you did. You can ask God to forgive you and tell yourself this truth: "Jesus died on the cross for my sins, even this sin of hurting Rhonda. For His sake, God forgives me so I don't have to feel awful or guilty. And I can tell myself the truth next time. God loves me and gives me new chances when I blow it."

MURIEL: So I get a new start! Even if I don't *always* tell myself the truth or do the right thing, it's not the end of the world, is it? And I can go over and tell Rhonda I'd like her to play with me. She and I might get to be good friends!

Such conversations must be conducted by parents who are open and frank about their own sinfulness, misbeliefs, and failures, not pompous fakes who talk down to children. When we discuss temptation, success, and failure with each other, remember, we are all sinners who come short of perfection and need daily renewal through the power of Christ's atonement!

Using one of the imaginary situations your children have come up with, role-play with them. You might take the role of tempting self-talk and the child truthful self-talk. Siblings can also learn about self-control by playing other roles.

Learning Self-control in Advance Planning

Children can develop resistance to temptation but still score low on other facets of self-control. They need to take all the courses in God's training school. It's not enough to pass one subject victoriously and flunk the others. For instance, a child who never cheats or steals may always be late in finishing any task.

To help children learn planning and foresight, start by telling a story something like this:

Once upon a time there was a boy named Lee whose brain was hooked up so that he couldn't think about anything unless it had already happened. When people asked Lee, "What are you going to do tomorrow?" he would invariably respond, "I don't know. I'll wait and see." When it was time to go to church or to school, he was never ready. He hadn't remembered to wash his face or comb his hair, so he had to hurry. It seemed as though most of the time he was racing and puffing and panting. Even so, he was always late. He was late getting to school. He was late getting to Sunday school. He was late getting to church. He was late arriving at his friends' birthday parties. He was late wherever he went. When his dad had a birthday, he never thought to make him a card or give him a present. His mom went to the hospital for an operation, but he didn't think about writing her a note to tell her he hoped she would get well. When it was time to pray, he couldn't think ahead so he couldn't think of anything to pray for.

Sometimes the kids in the neighborhood sat around talking about the future. They chatted about what they were going to do Saturday or what they wanted to be when they grew up. Sometimes they told what sports they might like to play when they went to high school. At those times, Lee couldn't think of anything to talk about. He wanted to run and climb trees and dig caves under the ground.

One day Lee's mother and father had a talk.

"I'm worried," said Dad. "Lee's brain is hooked up so he can't think ahead or plan anything."

"I'm worried, too," said Lee's mom. "Lee can't go to high school or college or even get a very good job unless he can think and plan. What can we do to help his brain rewire itself so he can think about tomorrow?"

"I have an idea," said Lee's dad. "Why don't we *teach* him how to plan?"

"That's a great idea," said Lee's mom. "We can show him how today is yesterday's tomorrow."

"Yes, indeed! That will help him understand why it's important to plan," said her husband.

"Maybe we could start by telling him the tale of the ant and the grasshopper," Lee's mother suggested.

So Lee's father called him and said, "Lee, I have a story to tell you. Listen. On a sunny day in summer a grasshopper was hopping about a field, singing happily, when an ant came by, slowly carrying a grain of corn to his home. 'Come and talk to me,' invited the grasshopper. 'Let's sing and skip and have fun.' 'No,' replied the ant, 'I am putting away food for the long, cold winter. You should do the same, so you too will have food later on.' 'Oh, winter is a long way off,' said the grasshopper. 'There is plenty to eat now.' And he went skipping over the meadow, humming merrily. The ant went on his way. All summer long he worked, while the idle grasshopper played and played. But when winter came the grasshopper had no food. He was so hungry that he had to beg food from the ants, who had corn and grain every day because they had saved it during the summer."[1]

"Did the ants help the grasshopper?" Lee asked.

"I don't know," replied his father, "but I wouldn't count on it. The grasshopper should have learned to plan so he wouldn't have to beg and depend on the ants. We all need to be able to plan to avoid trouble."

"For instance," said Mother, "how could you plan ahead so you could catch the school bus on time tomorrow without having to rush and pant and puff? Planning is the same as closing your eyes and pretending—like playing a game. You pretend it's tomorrow morning and pretend you are doing what you need to do to catch the bus without having to hurry," she explained.

Lee tried pretending it was tomorrow. That was easy, so he tried pretending it was Christmas. That was fun. He found that when he played the pretend game, he could think about any day he chose! After that, Lee and his parents talked about planning ahead, and Lee began to put the idea into practice. They talked together at the dinner table almost every night about what Lee had been planning and doing. And you'll be glad to hear that Lee's brain gradually rewired itself so he could think and plan just like other people.

After telling the story of Lee, follow up with a specific question. For example, ask, "What could you do to make sure you catch the school bus at exactly 7:30 in the morning without having to rush or go to school hungry?" After the child outlines a realistic morning schedule, discuss self-talk and how to develop new self-instructions. To help the child with self-talk, ask, "What do you think you will be telling yourself tomorrow when it's six o'clock and the alarm rings?" Wait while the child imagines tomorrow and tries to answer.

Stories are excellent, but children need to understand the point of any stories used. Good stories will naturally reveal their point and lead to questions and discussion.

Jesus' tale about the young women who forgot the oil for their wedding lamps is another good story to use (Matthew 25:1–13). It very powerfully makes the point about planning.

Parents should help their children realistically face the problem of planning. Most children will have self-talk thoughts about six o'clock alarms such as, "It's snug and warm in my bed and cold in the house. I'm going to turn over and sleep just a few minutes more." Another might be, "I'm not hungry, so I can skip breakfast and stay in bed a little longer." They might tell themselves, "I won't take a shower because I didn't get very dirty yesterday. I don't have to get up quite yet." They might think, "The bus will be late and I don't like waiting for it, so I'll stay here for just a minute or two more."

Parents can help children change their self-talk about wake-ups to the following: "I don't have to give up my plan to dress myself and eat and get to the bus on time. I know how to talk back to my old stalling tactics. Yes, I probably would enjoy sleeping longer. But it's more important to get my hair fixed right. I don't want to spend all day with hair problems." "I need to get a good breakfast so I won't feel hollow inside." "I want to take a good shower so I'll feel fresh and clean. I'm going to stick to the plan."

Asking, "How would you plan your birthday party?" can kick off an exciting exercise in foresight and planning for a small child (or an older one for that matter). "How many people would you invite? What would you like to do at your party? Which day of the week would be best? What time? Why do you think so?"

"What would your self-talk probably sound like if you felt like not finishing your homework? What would you say to get yourself to look ahead at the results? If you felt like not practicing the piano, or not doing your chores?"

Role-play, with each of you playing a self-talk part. You can switch off playing the roles of the child's old self-talk and his new foresight-orientated self-talk. Teach the child to internalize his new self-talk by taking these steps:

1. Say it aloud!

2. Whisper it to yourself!
3. Think it in your head!
4. Reward yourself!

Check with the young child to make certain she has really done #3. She should repeat the whole self-talk speech in her head, not merely a portion of it.

Self-reinforcement

When children control themselves, resist temptation, or carry out a plan, the behavior needs to be reinforced. Parents can help their children listen for the voice of their Father in heaven saying, "Well done!" Children can say to themselves, "Thank you, Lord! I did it with your help!" or "I controlled my anger. I did get mad at that kid, but I told myself not to hit him and I didn't! I put up with the frustrating feelings and they went away." "Planning ahead paid off! I got my history paper done a day early. Wow! I feel good about it, too." Children should practice rehearsing or role-playing similar self-reinforcement phrases.

We all have a deep sense of satisfaction when we maintain self-control. In Christians, this sense of fulfillment need not be pride or self-adulation; it can be truthful awareness of having done what is pleasing to God. We know when we have done a good job. Self-reinforcement encourages us to continue. We may think this step is unnecessary or unimportant, but the effect of self-reinforcement has been demonstrated. And it is especially vital for youngsters to learn how to do it.

Failure

Every plan to improve behavior should include a provision for what to do in case of a relapse or failure. Children need to learn to tell themselves the truth in case of failure: "It's not the end of the world that I didn't do it perfectly this time. I'll just learn from this and try harder next time! I want to obey the rules. I want to be responsible. I want to hang in there. I'm not going to quit trying. I'm going to ask God to take over my will. I will go over the steps I have learned and teach myself to do what I really want to do."

Self-control isn't such a mystery. It involves resisting temptation with God's help and being prepared by planning ahead. The essence of self-control is truth. Teaching and modeling the self-talk that leads to self-control will help your children succeed.

11

The Bottom Line

Solving Problems With the Truth

Ordinary kids face problems all the time. Most parents have had to deal with at least some of the following:

Mary has to play alone because neither side wants her to play on their team.

Johnny has new glasses. Kids tease him, calling him "four-eyes."

Susy's classmates ridiculed her because of the "dumb" answer she offered.

Daniel forgot to study. The test is this morning.

The captain of the football team offered Jennifer a can of beer at the party.

David's friends called him a eunuch because he wouldn't go to bed with Lori.

Amy's grades are mostly D's because she hasn't been turning in her homework assignments for most of the semester.

Do You Give Answers or Teach Skills?

A friend told us she made the mistake of giving her sons ready-made solutions to their problems instead of helping them reach their own conclusions. Most parents, like our friend, rush to give kids the answers. Sometimes they do this because they love their kids so much and want them to come out on top! But is it the best way to help? We don't think so. Why? Because they could instead teach their children problem-solving skills that would be useful throughout their lives. Isn't that wiser than giving answers useful only for the immediate problem?

Some parents imagine that their children are incapable of working through a problem and arriving at a solution. Such parents think they have been put on earth to give their children directions. "My children? Solve problems? They're too young! They still need to be told what to do."

On the contrary, youngsters can be trained to solve problems. Even very young children can gain the necessary proficiencies. Research has revealed that youngsters who get the opportunity to tackle problems systematically have tremendous advantages over other children. These advantages include superior coping skills, ability to handle life's frustrations, reduced levels of stress, and better academic performance. Perhaps the most significant outcome for children is a reduced likelihood of becoming delinquent, abusing drugs or alcohol, or developing psychological difficulties.[1]

The Steps in Problem-Solving

Following are some problem-solving steps psychologists have devised. We have added Step 4 because without God's approval and direction, even the best-laid plans can go awry, as we parents know so well. These procedures are simple and easy to learn.[2] (See the Appendix for charts you can use and copy.)

You will have to work through these steps many times with your children before they are able to complete the procedure on their own. Doing so takes more time than simply telling them what to do, but it takes less time than dealing with a wayward adolescent. Many teens get into trouble because they were never taught effective problem-solving techniques. Thus, when problems arise, they deal with them the best way they can think of. Unfortunately, it is often illegal or socially unacceptable.

Step 1: STOP! Ask—What is the problem? Interrupt impulsive reactions whenever possible, help the child calm down, and then think through the situation together. Identify the problem by asking questions until you understand what your child is saying to himself or herself. Is it truthful?

Step 2: THINK! What can be done about the problem? Have your child think of all the possible solutions for handling the difficulty. Write them down if it is feasible.

Step 3: CHOOSE! Help your child consider the likely consequences of each solution and select the one with the best outcome. Put a star next to the best plan.

Step 4: CHECK! Will God like this? Some solutions may go against what God has said in the Bible. Children should learn to check their solutions with the Bible and their parents.

Step 5: ACT! Try the solution.

Step 6: REVIEW! Did the solution work? If it did, the problem is solved. If it didn't, try another solution from Step 2 and repeat Steps 4–6.

Noticing Signals

Making your way through life can be tricky! A person learning to drive has to learn to watch for and interpret signals. A flashing red light means one thing; a continuous red light means something else. Signals within the person and signals transmitted by others often contain valuable information. Teach children to notice such signals. Paying attention to them will help youngsters to safely and successfully negotiate life's curves.

Problem-solving proceeds best when children learn to read their own internal signals. Those internal cues are feelings and thoughts. Mr. Searchbrain, the thought detective, can help young children pay attention to their own signals as well as to the signals others beam to them. You might say something like, "Mr. Searchbrain wants to help you solve the case like a real detective. He'd like to help you look at what is going on in your feelings and thoughts. Maybe you can detect some signals."

Mr. Searchbrain can ask children, "How are you feeling right now?" Painful feelings like anger, sadness, or nervousness usually are the first inkling of a problem. Then Mr. Searchbrain might suggest that they pay attention to their thoughts about the feelings. Children can ask themselves about their own thoughts. "What is going through my head right now? What am I thinking about myself, about others, about what's happening?" Becoming aware of internal speech or self-talk will help children identify the problem. By thinking carefully, they can usually come up with some possible solutions, figure out probable consequences of each, choose the one most likely to work, and determine a plan to carry it out.

Finally, they should attend to the signals received from their bodies. "What are you feeling in your body right now?" Mr. Searchbrain might query. Tense muscles, rapid heartbeat, sweating, butterflies in the stomach, and other bodily sensations might say something about the problem.

Using Stories to Solve Problems With Younger Children

One of the best ways to teach younger children problem-solving skills is to tell them stories. Make up tales of children who have ordinary childhood problems. Tell how they worked with Mr. Searchbrain to understand their difficulties and how they carried out the six steps to arrive at solutions. For example, a parent might tell the story of how Mr. Searchbrain helped Ashley work through a problem. Ashley's best friend, Theresa, was hanging around with another classmate, Tammie, and Ashley felt left out and hurt.

MR. SEARCHBRAIN: Why are you so upset, ASHLEY? (Step 1: Stop!)

ASHLEY: Theresa was spending more time with Tammie than with me.

MR. SEARCHBRAIN: What could you do about it? (Step 2: Think!)

ASHLEY: Well, I could cry and make them feel sorry for me. I could get really mad and tell them off. I could ignore them and find someone else to play with. I could play with the two of them. Or I could just play by myself.

MR. SEARCHBRAIN: What do you think is the best thing to do? (Step 3: Choose!) What will happen if you cry?

ASHLEY: I'll look like a baby.

MR. SEARCHBRAIN: What will happen if you get mad and tell them off?

ASHLEY: They might get mad and never want to play with me again.

MR. SEARCHBRAIN: What will happen if you ignore them and find someone else to play with?

ASHLEY: They won't know what to think, but I'll have a new friend.

MR. SEARCHBRAIN: What will happen if you try to play with them?

ASHLEY: They might say something mean like "three's a crowd." Then I'd feel even worse.

MR. SEARCHBRAIN: What will happen if you play by yourself?

ASHLEY: I'll feel lonely.

MR. SEARCHBRAIN: So which is the best solution?

ASHLEY: Find someone else to play with.

MR. SEARCHBRAIN: Do you think God would like that idea? (Step 4: Check!)

ASHLEY: Well, He probably wouldn't want me to cry or yell at them. But He probably wouldn't mind if I played by myself, tried playing with them, or found someone else to play with. So, yeah, I think He'd approve of my choice.

MR. SEARCHBRAIN: So what are you going to do next?
(Step 5: Act!)
ASHLEY: Find someone else to play with.
MR. SEARCHBRAIN: Are you satisfied with the solution?
(Step 6: Review!)
ASHLEY: Yes! It worked!

Problem-Solving With Older Children

Parents can use the same steps with older children, though the approach may be different. They may want to review the steps and then let their children go through the process themselves. Or they might want to tell them about fifteen-year-old Tommy who was earning a D average in tenth grade. The second semester was nearly over, and his parents were definitely not amused by his grades. They finally told him that if he didn't pull his grades up to at least a B average, he wouldn't be allowed to take driver's ed this coming summer. Time was running out. Tommy had been taught as a child to use the problem-solving steps we've been talking about, so he had the following conversation with himself. Adapt the story as necessary to use with your own child.

"First, I've got to STOP and figure out the problem. That's easy. The problem is my grades! I've been having fun and playing around for two semesters. Now Mom and Dad are really upset. They're serious about my license, too. I won't get a driver's permit if I don't get these dumb grades up. The problem is I'd rather bum around than study. I've been telling myself something that isn't really true—that having fun is the most important thing in life. It's not really what life is all about, I guess.

"Second, I've got to THINK! What are some solutions? That's not so easy. I suppose I could do some heavy cheating on the tests. Or, I could keep doing what I've been doing and not get my driver's permit. Besides, there's always next year. Or I could stay home evenings and work to get my grades up to at least a B. Or maybe I could see if Ted's family would adopt me. They're really easy on Ted; they'd let me get my permit, no matter how bad my grades are.

"Third, I've got to CHOOSE! What is the best solution? Well, if I cheat I might get by with it, but I might get caught. Then I'd be in even more trouble. My dad probably would never let me get my driver's license. Besides, even if I could cheat on the tests, there's still homework to hand in. If I just keep doing what I've been doing and forget my permit, the guys won't let me forget it!

"And then there's Jennifer. She'll drop me for sure if I don't learn to drive! If I give it my best shot and try to pull up these grades, I won't be able to watch much TV or hang out with the guys. I'll have to work and put the other stuff off for a while. Ted's family probably wouldn't adopt me anyway. They do like me, but they'd for sure stick by my parents. I guess the best plan is the hardest one: work on getting my grades up.

"Fourth, I've got to CHECK my solution against God's Word. What would He have to say? Well, God would never approve of cheating, that's for sure. And, I guess the truth is that God would prefer if I goofed off less. Besides, He usually sees eye to eye with my parents, and Mom and Dad do want my best. They're not too bad! I guess God gave them to me, though there are times when I wonder about His judgment! Seriously, though, obedience to Him is the way to go. There's no doubt about what's pleasing to God: hard work. I'm going to give it my best shot!

"Fifth, here we come to the hard part. Now I've got to ACT! I have to try out my solution. It doesn't sound like much fun, but I'll work to get my grades up. I know with God's help I can do it, and I'll probably feel a lot better about myself when it's all over. Besides, I just have to have that driver's permit!

"Phew! Those two months are finally behind me. Now I get to REVIEW my solution. Did it work? Yup, it sure did. I had to practically turn into a hermit for two months to catch up. It wasn't easy, but I did it. Now I can get my permit. And another thing, I know how to study now, so I think I'll be able to get into a good university when I graduate."

Be sure to encourage your teen, and even younger children, to write out the steps in problem-solving. Seeing the problem, the signals, the proposed solutions, the consequences, and the test for pleasing God written out can aid clarity of thinking. Younger children will need more help in evaluating the pros and cons of their decisions. Young children usually have simplistic and rigid notions of good and bad, right and wrong, and can use a good deal of adult help in reaching decisions. Older elementary kids are eager to find and use problem-solving skills. They are becoming more independent, so they want to do things for themselves. These youngsters also begin to want to handle their own problems. They will spend less time in adult company and require less direct adult supervision. Teenagers are quite sophisticated in their abstract-thinking abilities. The often contradictory pressures of family standards and peer codes create dilemmas for these kids. Learning to solve problems can be invaluable for them.

Eventually, with practice, all children will find problem-solving second nature and there will be little need to write out the steps every time. (See the worksheet in the Appendix.)

Typically, younger children make decisions with little forethought and change their decisions or forget them readily. As children get older, they should learn to give careful thought to decisions and make them in the light of the truth. Here are steps to be followed when the problem involves making a decision:

- Clearly state the decision to be made.
- List advantages of each.
- Rate each advantage with a number (1–5):
  (1) Not too important: 1 or 2
  (2) Somewhat important: 3
  (3) Very important: 4 or 5
- Add up numbers for pros and cons separately.
- The choice with the highest total should be the one selected.

Problems are a normal part of life. Learning to solve

them at an early age provides skills forever.

When conflict arises, children need to be trained to STOP and THINK! Among the cues they need to look for are FEELINGS and then THOUGHTS; they exist in all problems. Are they truthful? If so, follow them. If not, find out what is truthful and act accordingly. And practice, practice, practice. It is imperative to practice.

12

"To Tell You the Truth . . ."

Learning to Communicate Honestly

Marlys wept. Looking out the window, she saw eight-year-old Gary sitting on the curb, alone and forlorn. The sound of shouts and whoops of delight coming from the neighborhood kids playing ball down the street deepened her misery over her son's sad isolation. She knew he needed to be with them. Why wouldn't they ask him to play?

For a young parent, a rejected child's hurt feelings and lonely isolation bring agony and a sense of utter helplessness. Gary withdrew more every day into a secret inner shelter. But seeking comfort in himself and in his own day-dreams only increased his loneliness and alienation.

"What can I do to help him?" Marlys asked herself daily. But no one ever answered her.

Many parents have felt baffled by a beautiful child's social inadequacy. Sometimes the situation improves if it is due only to a temporary disagreement with peers. But sometimes the problem gets out of hand, and even the most conscientious parents can't think of anything they can do to help.

Concentrate on Communication Skills

There are many factors that contribute to loneliness in children, but isolation usually results from poor communication skills. And parents *can* do something about that.

We have solid evidence showing that kids with poor communication skills are less liked by peers, while those with good communication skills are popular. Furthermore, and this is the most important finding, when children receive training in conversation and social skills, their popularity *increases*.[1]

By communication skills we do not mean merely the ability to talk. Although communication skills involve speech, they include other skills as well, such as relational and social skills, as the following lists indicate:

Popular kids are proficient at the following communication skills:

• Knowing how to listen to others.
• Looking other people in the eye and repeatedly renewing eye contact.
• Asking questions of others.
• Giving truthful compliments to others and receiving truthful compliments graciously.
• Knowing how to share and sensing when sharing is a good idea.
• Making an effort to understand another person's point of view.
• Knowing how to use these skills in relationships with peers and adults.

Unpopular children display traits that alienate others:

• Unpopular children display traits that alienate others.
• Getting distracted when another person is talking.
• Avoiding eye contact, looking down or looking around instead of returning the gaze of the other person.
• Interrupting the person who is talking.
• Acting selfishly, refusing to share or to consider others' wishes.

- Understanding only their own point of view and making no effort to understand that of others.
- Exhibiting poor interpersonal habits in their relationships with peers and adults.

These lists reveal that popular youngsters habitually reward others for associating with them while unpopular youngsters seldom give others social rewards. It is astonishing to see how the lists compare with the fruit of the Spirit and the works of the flesh described by the apostle Paul in Galatians 5.

Listening, the Essential Ingredient

What single ingredient contributes most toward good social skills? *Listening!* When children *really hear* what another person is saying, they can respond appropriately. When their attention is riveted on *their own* wishes, *their own* concerns, getting *their own* way, and on what *they* want to say next, they can't respond appropriately. They fail to reward the other person, and as a result they find themselves isolated.

Teach your children the following listening skills:

- *Look* at the person who is talking.
- *Think* about what that person is saying.
- *Nod, smile,* change facial expressions; react to what is being said.
- *Don't interrupt!*
- *Pretend* you are the other person. Try to figure out what he or she feels, thinks, wants, means.

Kindness and Consideration Sum It All Up

Positive social skills embody truthfulness, kindness, and thoughtfulness. Pay attention to good conversationalists. Notice that they do the following considerate things:

- Ask questions and/or tell something about themselves.

- Listen to what the other person says and respond intelligently and thoughtfully.
- Continue the interaction by asking another question and/or telling something more about themselves, relating it to what the other person just said.
- Take turns, not monopolizing the conversation.
- When ending the conversation, they wait for the other person to stop talking. Then they say they have to leave and explain why and mention a time when they might talk later.

How Do Children Learn to Communicate?

Listening skills sometimes seem manipulative. Learning them may seem less than genuine and truthful. In fact, everything in this chapter might come off that way. But remember, the Holy Spirit dwells in the hearts of Christians to anchor social behaviors in the truth and love of God. The communication skills we describe, when done in truth, reflect the fruit of the Spirit.

Christian children as well as adults have the Holy Spirit prompting them to be loving and truthful when they listen and converse. But while some children have superb social skills, others display few skills and many unappealing habits in social contexts. Why? Where do children acquire social skills? What other forces, besides the counsel of God's indwelling Spirit, shape social behavior?

One major factor is *learning,* and most kids learn these habits from their parents! They observe and imitate you. If you see bad habits in your child, look at your own social behavior. Please don't be offended. We aren't saying that you are a social dud if your child has trouble with peers. We do, however, suggest that you examine yourself. Do you listen, give intelligent feedback, avoid interrupting, look the speaker in the eye, ask thoughtful questions, give and receive compliments sincerely and graciously, share appropriately, and try hard to grasp the other person's viewpoint?

If you can honestly answer yes to all the above, congratulations. You score high. But if you (sometimes) interrupt others, talk when they are speaking, think about other things when someone else is speaking, fail to look the speaker in the eye, and want to be understood more than you want to understand, you too have a communication deficiency. But don't despair. Most of us fall somewhere between these extreme descriptions. The necessary thing is to face the truth without flinching. You may discover that your child's faulty social habits were learned from you or from your mate.

We have, however, seen instances in which parents who were adept at interpersonal relationships, for some unfathomable reason, had offspring who were unable to communicate. We have also seen the opposite: parents who were quiet, introverted, and isolated with children who seemed to know instinctively how to relate to others. In psychology, there are enough exceptions to the rule to keep the experts humble.

Working Together on Improvement

However you explain your child's communication habits, it is good for the whole family to work on improvement. One of the best occasions for practice might be at the dinner table. Choose a time when everyone is relaxed, not when parent-child misunderstandings need to be worked through.

Frank and Beth considered it worth a try. They had serious concerns about the isolation of nine-year-old Alan. Alan's teacher had often expressed her concern about him. He usually kept to himself or played with the second- and third-graders. He seldom spent time with his fourth-grade peers. In Alan's interactions with younger children, he insisted on doing the talking. He monopolized the play equipment and refused to let others have turns. He frequently out-shouted others and forced conversations to dwell exclusively on his interests. Beth had noticed that Alan hardly ever talked about friends. He never asked to visit anyone or to have anyone visit him. Most of his time he spent alone watching TV or riding his bike. When she suggested that he might like to invite a friend over, he shrugged.

Neither Frank nor Beth could get Alan to discuss the problem, but that is not unusual. Children can seldom be prompted to confront a problem head on or even to present a problem in the same straightforward way as the typical adult does.

So Beth and Frank sought professional advice. Following Dr. Clarkson's suggestions, they decided to turn dinner time into training sessions. Instead of asking Alan to discuss the problem of his social behavior, Frank simply announced that the family would learn the proper way to converse with other people.

They began by reading what God has to say about the fruit of the Spirit. Here is what they read and discussed during their first session:

> The fruit of the Spirit is love, joy, peace, patience, kindness, goodness, faithfulness, gentleness, self-control; against such there is no law. And those who belong to Christ Jesus have crucified the flesh with its passions and desires. If we live by the Spirit, let us also walk by the Spirit. Let us have no self-conceit, no provoking of one another, no envy of one another (Galatians 5:22–26).

They talked about how their dealings with others could be more loving. They asked God to show them how and when their treatment of other people was self-centered. They compared their behavior to the social behaviors listed above. Sometimes their behavior more closely resembled that of rejected kids. In other instances, it was more like that of popular kids. And they saw clearly that the fruit of the Spirit closely resembles the behavior found among socially skilled people. The traits of poor conversationalists apparently come more from the flesh than from the Spirit.

When they first discussed examples of both kinds of behavior, Alan identified conceit, provocative behavior, and envy only in others. As they continued talking, however, and particularly as Frank and Beth set the example, Alan joined his parents in looking truthfully at his own behavior. They came to realize that their conversations with others were sometimes self-centered and fleshly rather than other-centered and Spirit-directed.

But the family didn't stop with discussion. They practiced new, more loving, kinder communication habits with one another. First, Frank would role-play a conversation with Beth. Alan would watch and listen and call attention to behavior he thought they could improve. Then Alan and Beth would role-play and Frank would suggest changes he thought would be useful. Then Alan and Frank took the stage and Beth served as the audience-coach. Here is an example of one of their role-play conversations. Frank set the scene:

"You and I are kids in school, Beth, and we're sitting in the cafeteria having lunch. You play it straight and I'll purposely break all the rules for being a good communicator. OK?"

Beth agreed and she opened the conversation:

BETH: Hey, Frank, what did your mom put in your sandwich? I got peanut butter and jam in mine. Want to trade?

FRANK: Yuk! I hate peanut butter. And your sandwich looks yucky. I got turkey in mine. I'm not gonna trade—no way.

BETH: Oh. OK. Guess what? We went to the beach yesterday and you won't believe what we saw! A great big fin sticking out of the water—we were pretty sure it was a shark so we got out of there fast. We played in the sand for a while and . . .

FRANK: (who has been looking all around the room, giving Beth no eye contact at all.) I hate peanut butter. My mom puts it in my lunch sometimes and it's dumb. I can ride a two-wheeler and I'm gonna get one for my birthday. Then I'm gonna ride it to school every day, and maybe I'll take some trips on it, too. My big brother rides all the way to Gurneyville and back. Maybe I will, too.

BETH: Lucky! I'll bet you're a good bike-rider. I'd like to get a two-wheeler. Can I have a ride on yours when you get it?

FRANK: (still looking around the room, down at his lunch, anywhere but at Beth.) I'm gonna get a trail bike. They have trail bikes now that have big tires instead of those thin ones. I'm gonna get one with big tires.

After the role-play, Alan told his father he needed to improve the following things: He should look Beth in the eye instead of gaze around the room; he should not insult Beth's lunch; if he didn't want to share he should politely decline her offer; he should show interest in Beth's experience at the beach and answer her request to ride his new bike. It was wrong for him to force the conversation onto his subject and to ignore Beth's interests.

Next, Alan took Frank's place. But this time Alan was to show better social behavior. Beth kept her role, and they tried the lunchtime conversation again. Here is how it went the second time:

BETH: Hey, Alan, what did your mom put in your sandwich? I got peanut butter and jam in mine. Want to trade?

ALAN: Mmm. I'll trade a half with you. Let's see. Mine's turkey. Do you like turkey? It's on my grandpa's fresh baked bread. And I've got M&Ms too. This is going to be a go-o-od lunch. Want some?

BETH: Sure. Thanks. Mmm. Looks good. My grandpa doesn't bake bread. How come yours does?

ALAN: Oh, he does all kinds of things. I never know what he's going to do next. He writes stories for me, too, for my very own book. What kinds of things does yours do?

BETH: Well, he plays golf a lot. He's going to teach me how and even give me some golf clubs when I get a little older. He took my family to the beach yesterday and guess what? We saw a great big fin sticking out of the water—we were pretty sure it was a shark so we got out of there fast. We played in the sand for a while and built some neat sandcastles and stuff. My dad built a really funny one.

ALAN: (looking Beth in the eye) Did the shark go away? You must have been scared! I bet you guys didn't go back in the water, did you?

BETH: Yeah, we did. The lifeguard told us the fin was from a dolphin, not a shark, and dolphins like people. They don't hurt anybody. Do you go swimming in the ocean?

ALAN: Sure, sometimes. And we build sandcastles, too. My dad helped us work on one once that took up most of the beach! It was huge!

BETH: Sounds like you have fun at the beach, too. I have to go get in the jump rope line now. Talk to you tomorrow.

ALAN: See you at lunch!

Frank thought Alan and Beth both did very well. They asked each other questions and shared information too. Each one listened to the other. Their replies were related to what the other person had just said. Beth waited for Alan to finish a sentence before she ended their conversation, telling why she had to leave, and both agreed to talk later.

What to Practice

When you role-play and coach one another in your family practice sessions, improvement may not come as fast as in our abbreviated example above. You will need to work on specific tactics and skills, such as asking questions, asking someone to share with you, and making different types of requests. Remember these pointers about requests and questions:

1. *Decide:* What is it you want or need? What is it you want to know?
2. *Wait:* Choose a good time to ask (not when the other person is concentrating on something important, talking, or not feeling well).

3. *Think:* Come up with a courteous way to say what you want to say.
4. *Respond:* Say "Thank you" and express appreciation with other appropriate phrases.

Practice giving and receiving compliments. Graciousness doesn't come easily to everyone. Truthful and purposeful compliments have an important place among communication skills. Remember to teach your children these things:

1. *Be aware.* Know what others are doing. Notice if someone is especially kind and thoughtful.
2. *Let the other person know.* Tell the other person you appreciate what he or she did. "I really like the picture you drew!" or, "You played a good game today. Way to go!"
3. *Receive compliments graciously.* If giving compliments seems difficult, receiving one can be even more so. Some people have a habit of denying the truth of compliments. "No, I didn't play very well at all," or, "It's really not a very good drawing. Most of mine are much better." Encourage your children to say a simple "Thank you" when someone compliments them. Then they can decide if they want to add anything. It makes the other person believe their compliment was taken seriously if you say something like, "I'm really glad you liked my drawing. I worked on it all weekend," or, "It means a lot to me that you think I did well."
4. *NEVER say negative things about your performance!* It only draws attention to yourself and points out your insecurities. It may also be untruthful and come across as false humility. Even if you think the compliment is exaggerated, a negative response will make the person who complimented you feel put down because, in essence, you are saying, "You're wrong." Teach your children that it is all right to be good at something and that it is not prideful to accept that as a fact. It is fine to be successful and to accept compliments with gratitude. Some children are led to believe it is shameful to accept a compliment as true.

See the Appendix for more help in practicing social skills.

When Families Work on Communication

Here are some do's and don'ts for families working to improve their communication skills:

DO

- Use brief statements of ten words or less and then pause so others have a chance to join the conversation.
- Use "I" statements like "I feel . . ." or "I like it when . . ."
- Use specific statements that tell the listener exactly what you mean. For example, "I want you to stop teasing your sister!" instead of, "Don't you think you could stop teasing your sister now?"
- Use active listening skills: Maintain good eye contact, lean forward, nod when appropriate, smile, be responsive.
- Let others state their thoughts completely before stating yours.
- Give feedback. Paraphrase what the other person said to make sure you really understood. "You seem to be telling me that . . ."
- Be constructive. Instead of saying, "You'd better get good grades starting tomorrow!" say, "I'm concerned about your grades. Let's figure out some way to pull them up," or, "Something is bothering you. Can we discuss it?"
- Use a neutral, natural tone of voice.
- Stay on one topic.
- Focus on the here and now.
- Make sure there is congruence between verbal and nonverbal communication. For example, smile when you say "I love you."
- Express feelings appropriately.
- Use appropriate facial expressions.

DON'T

- Extend your speeches into long lectures or sermons.
- Blame others by saying, "You are the problem here," or, "It's all your fault that this happened."
- Make vague statements like, "Just shape up!" or "Knock it off!"
- Look away from others, give the silent treatment, cross your arms, interrupt, or cover your face.
- Use put-downs like, "You're worthless!" or "I'm sick of you!" Don't use threats like, "I'm going to make you sorry if you do that." Don't be sarcastic. Don't yell.
- Go from subject to subject.
- Bring up a list of old issues or past bad behaviors.
- Create incongruence between verbal and nonverbal communications. For example, don't say, "I'm glad you did that," while pounding your fist angrily on a table.
- Keep feelings inside or try to hide them even if they are wrong.
- Scowl or use antagonistic facial expressions.

All families have problems. Taking the time to learn family problem-solving is well worth the investment. Here's how it's done:

Family Problem-Solving

You have learned how to teach your kids to solve problems. Why not use problem-solving for family issues?

1. Stop! What is the problem we're having?

As you attempt to formulate the problem, avoid blaming individuals. Instead, focus on how each member is interacting with the others to create the problem. For example, don't say, "We're late for church again because Mary wasn't ready on time!" Rather, "We have a problem being late for church because we didn't plan when we would start getting ready, how long it would take, and how early we would have to leave to get to church on time!" Agree on the way you state the problem.

2. *What are some plans we might use?*

Brainstorm. Don't evaluate or criticize anybody's ideas or suggestions. Instead, think together about as many alternatives as possible. Don't even consider how any of the suggestions might work out until you have generated several alternatives.

3. *What is the best plan we could use?*

After the alternatives have been listed, think of what would happen if the family followed each. How would each family member feel about the results of each alternative? Decide which alternative is most likely to succeed and meet the appropriate needs or goals of each person. Reach an agreement acceptable to most or, if possible, to all.

4. *Is our plan God-pleasing?*

We don't think this step should be omitted, even if you think the chance of your family's adopting a plan contrary to one of the Ten Commandments is very slim. Why? Because it focuses everyone's attention on the thing we seek first: God's kingdom and God's righteousness. And, of course, if the plan does include elements contrary to God's expressed will, this step insures against adopting it.

5. *Do the plan.*

Try working the plan as best the family can. Don't criticize and say, "I told you so." Be constructive. Give it your best shot.

6. *Did the plan work?*

Evaluate and find out if everyone is satisfied with the way the problem was solved. If the solution didn't work out or if some members have serious difficulties with it, go through the family problem-solving process again.

Be sure to stay focused on the here and now. Don't bring up old issues when you are trying to work out solutions to current difficulties. Old issues can prompt repeating old arguments. Soon the group forgets it was trying to solve a problem.

The Appendix contains a Family Problem-Solving worksheet that may be helpful to you.

In summary: Knowing how to converse and communicate will contribute to truthful self-esteem. There are wrong and right ways to communicate. Remember, the loving way to communicate involves acting truthfully and graciously toward others. Bring out the best in the other person as you communicate because the Holy Spirit gives you love for others!

Knowing how to communicate honestly and effectively will contribute to truthful self-esteem. There are wrong and right ways to communicate. The right way is lovingly, and that involves acting truthfully and graciously toward others. Children who learn early to express themselves truthfully, yet lovingly, will have a great advantage over others later in life.

13

Eyes on the Prize

Setting Truthful Goals and Standards

Twelve-year-old Peter could outrun everybody in school. He won all the running events with ease. Peter expected to win. In fact, it never occurred to him that he might lose. But when his family moved to a different city and Peter enrolled in seventh grade in a new school, he faced new competition. And he lost. He was no longer the best. Oh, he was still plenty good, but one boy was better. Peter found that intolerable. It hurt. He told himself he had to be the best, and being the best meant winning every race. Whenever he lost, Peter declared himself a failure. He thought about quitting the track team. Peter was angry and disgusted with himself because he had failed to live up to his standards.

"If I Don't Win, I'm a Failure"

Peter, like many other boys and girls, had never learned the truth about setting standards for himself. Nor had he learned to make his personal standards truthful. What does Peter's self-imposed rule—*I must always be the best or else I am a failure*—mean? Taken literally and without qualification, it means that Peter must run faster than anybody—even *Chariots of Fire* hero Eric Liddell, or any recent Olympic runner! According to Peter's standard, if anybody ever beats him, he must declare himself a failure.

What do we mean by "failure" when we apply it to a person rather than to an effort to achieve something? To be considered a true failure, a person would have to fail at everything. Someone who fails only once or twice can't honestly be considered a failure because he or she has at times succeeded. If one failure makes a person a failure, everybody who ever lived must be considered a failure because no one is always successful. Peter was telling himself nonsense. His rule was untruthful because it embodied misbeliefs. His frustration illustrates what youngsters experience when their standards are incompatible with truth and reality.

Goals Are Not Standards

Like us, our children have standards. Like ours, theirs may be unrealistically high or ridiculously low. A *standard* is an internal expectation we hold for ourselves (or for others). Standards may be based on our goals, but they are not goals. Goals are targets we try to reach; standards are rules for judging our performance. A goal gives us direction; a standard embodies our expectations.

Here are some examples of appropriate goals: "I will try to make three new friends." "I will keep my fingernails clean all the time." "I will be in bed by nine o'clock every night." "I will try to raise my grades from B's to A's."

Here are some examples of appropriate standards by which to evaluate our performance:

- Always make an effort. Encourage yourself when your efforts produce results.("Although I made only one new friend, I'm pleased because she's a cool person, the best friend I ever had!")
- Get to bed by 9:00 most nights, but occasional delays are okay. ("I've gotten in bed by 9:00 eight of the last ten

nights. I'm doing much better than I was doing before I started working on this. One night Grandpa and Grandma were visiting, and it was right to stay up to see them.")

- Keep making progress. ("Mom noticed how clean my fingernails have been lately. I did have dirty nails one night after I came in because my friend and I were digging a cave, but I have been scrubbing my nails with a brush at least once every day.")
- Carry out your program, work on worthwhile goals, don't give up. ("My grades have gone down instead of up. I know I haven't been doing my homework very well because I've been spending more time with my friend. I'm going to ask my counselor for some advice. Maybe she can show me how to make a schedule.")

Sometimes our standards or expectations are explicit. Then we know what to consider acceptable levels of achievement. Other times we have unspoken or unwritten expectations. Some of these may not be based on the truth. Depending on our own emotional and mental state, these expectations may surface at the wrong time and cause us to be untruthful in evaluating ourselves. Explicit standards and truthful self-talk work best.

Finding the Lies

Peter certainly had unrealistic expectations about racing. When Peter's father helped him analyze his painful self-dissatisfaction, he saw the lies embraced in his self-statements. Peter decided to make an effort to replace the lies with the truth. He also changed his expectations to be more in line with his goals.

"What do I really want to achieve when I run?" he asked himself.

"Well, I really want to win every race," Peter had to admit. He couldn't, in all honesty, tell himself that he would just as soon lose! Peter's father then showed him that he could truthfully say winning races was his goal.

"But goals are not standards," said his father. "It's one thing to tell yourself you want to win (that is the truth), and quite another thing to tell yourself that if you don't come in first every time, you're a failure (that is *not* the truth). You don't need to change your goals, Peter, but you do need to make your standards truthful."

"I see what you mean!" exclaimed Peter. "I can't truthfully call myself a *failure* just because I didn't reach my goal. I can truthfully say only that I failed to win this time. If I try hard and put plenty of effort into the race, I'm going to consider myself successful even when I don't win." Peter began to feel better. Why? Because he made changes in his self-talk about goals and standards. He stopped making his goals into standards. He told himself:

1. My *goal* is to win every race if I can. If I win, I'll tell myself I reached my goal. If I lose, I'll accept the fact that I didn't reach my goal this time. But I won't have to tell myself I'm a failure because I lost a race.

2. My *standard* by which I judge myself will be to give it my best shot every time. Whether I win or lose, I will consider myself successful for trying my hardest. And I will stop making myself think I'm a failure in life if I lose one race (or even a dozen races). Even if for some reason I don't try very hard in a race, I won't tell myself I'm a failure. I'll tell myself I failed this time to live up to my standards, and then I'll try to do better next time.

Parents, Goals, and Standards

Peter's father asked the right questions, stimulating his son's own thinking about standards and goals. Parents play the largest role in setting children's standards and goals. Some parents, excellent in every other way, nevertheless suffer from the sin of pride. Congratulating themselves proudly for their children's achievements, they lean on their offspring, demanding success. They use their children's accomplishments for their own aggrandizement. They even may insist that their children fulfill impossible goals. If parents hold up an impossible goal as a standard, children may try to attain it to please them. But when they fail, and their mortified parents show their displeasure, the children will begin to believe they are failures. "I must succeed in everything I attempt, and if I don't, I'm a disappointment!" they reason. Carrying impossible standards around in their heads, they will repeatedly consider themselves failures, losers, and hopeless cases. They may keep trying without ever gaining satisfaction, or they might quit trying altogether to avoid more painful failures.

We recall a young woman with only average intelligence who had grown up with frustration. She learned to hate report cards because her mother had decreed that she *must* get perfect grades. For the girl, C's were reasonable grades. How she feared her mother's disgusted response to every report card. Though she felt like a knife had been twisted inside her, she couldn't do better than bring home an occasional B. She must, she concluded, be a real dud!

Parents should consider carefully whether their ambitious aims for their children are manifestations of their own sinful pride. Unrealistic performance demands can make children always feel defeated.

Parents Without Standards

Today some parents and teachers, reacting against the tendency to set unrealistic goals for children, refuse to set any standards or goals. While it is true that unrealistically high standards may lead to frequent failure, this response goes too far. Many children get the impression that they need not achieve anything except a high opinion of themselves ("positive self-esteem"). Parents and teachers have been told to praise and reward children whether they do well or not. Many have backed off from correcting any defects in their children's performance. They pronounce whatever half-hearted performance the child manages "wonderful." Partly because of this trend, American children consistently earn lower achievement scores in math and science than children in any other developed nation on earth.

Parents don't have to stop setting goals to avoid making their children feel like washouts. Children are crying out for truthful standards. They want to know how to judge their own performance realistically.

The Criterion Is Truth

When discussing goals with children, keep the goals truthful and realistic. Standards for evaluating performance should be based solidly on the truth and should be reasonable and realistic. Here are some helpful principles for setting truthful goals and standards:

- Has God commanded this? Some standards come directly from God's revealed will, such as obeying parents, telling the truth, loving other people, and taking care of God's creation. Anything commanded by God must have the highest priority! But some goals are not commanded by God. They may be desirable but are not divinely mandated. Children should be taught to distinguish one from the other.

- Is it consistent with the child's developmental level? Is the child's neuromuscular coordination ready for it? The father who proudly demands that his three-year-old son learn to hit a baseball disregards the truth about the child's developmental level. He may inflict emotional damage on his child by expecting too much too soon.

- Is it consistent with the child's natural abilities? Reality imposes its own constraints. If a youngster can't carry a tune, don't demand that she become a diva. If a child's only interest is engines and putting them together, don't insist that he become a novelist. Desperate parents once sent a failing college student to see us. He was majoring in business so he could eventually take over the family's highly successful hardware chain, but he just wasn't getting it. His grades were barely passing. Testing revealed that his abilities and interests in selling hardware were small. His strong fields were theology, philosophy, and the humanities. A change of majors and new career goals were gladly supported by his family. The switch led to high grades and the likelihood that he will enjoy a successful career as a university professor! Parents' visions, dreams, and abilities should not be the foundation of standards for children.

- Is it good for the child? If the standard or goal has no purpose other than to fulfill a parent's own lifelong dream, it is untruthful. Pushing it on a child could be wrong. A mother who wanted to be a nurse but couldn't afford the training might pressure her daughter into pursuing the career in her place. Why? Fulfillment for herself? Or for the good of the child? The answer might of course be either or both. But if she is only telling herself nursing would be good for her daughter, she fails to look the whole truth squarely in the face. If a goal enables a child to walk with God, socialize well, make and keep good friends, effectively pursue a career, and develop self-sufficiency, it is likely to be truthful.

- Is it good for others? A child should learn from parental teaching to adopt goals with a view toward loving and serving others. A human "environmental impact statement" should accompany the adoption of life goals with the aim of living for the good of others.

- Can the child accept the goal? Work with it? Agree with it? Goals should not just gratify a child's whims; they should be compatible with interests and abilities. It should be possible to discuss goals and standards with a child. Parents should give a little, get a little, and negotiate. A discussion with a child about goals and standards is important early in their development but especially near adolescence when peer pressures become enormous. As James Dobson has put it, "A kid's greatest anxiety, far exceeding fear of death, is the possibility of rejection or humiliation in the eyes of his peers. The ultimate danger will lurk in the background for years, motivating him to do things that make absolutely no sense to the adults who watch. It is impossible to comprehend the adolescent mind without understanding the terror of the peer group."[1]

Sometimes older kids may find themselves ostracized by their peers when they abandon the standards of their peer group in favor of their parents' values and standards. This is why we underline the importance of helping children establish good friends and peers. Parents can cultivate friendships with other parents who have children at the same school or church as their children. They can also socialize family to family. This gives children the opportunity to make friends with peers who have similar values.

Writing Down Goals and Standards

It is helpful for children and adolescents to write down their goals and standards. They can use almost the same steps as those for problem solving (Chapter 10). The steps might look like this:

Step 1: STOP! What is my goal?

Step 2: THINK! What steps do I need to take to reach my goal?

Step 3: CHECK! Will God like this goal?

Step 4: ACT! Carry out the program to reach the goal.

Step 5: REVIEW! Did my program work? Did I reach my goal?[2]

A Goals and Standards Questionnaire[3]

Dr. Kevin Stark has devised a questionnaire to help parents and kids find out what their own goals and standards are and whether they are meeting them. You and your children might want to check yourselves with it.

PART 1

Please read the following ten questions and answer them according to the way you would *like* to be. Tell how well you would need to do on each to feel truly good about yourself.

If you could do very poorly and still feel really good about yourself, put an X over the 0. If you would only need to come out average, put an X over the 5. And if you would have to do perfectly, put an X over the 10. If you would need to do better than average, put the X somewhere between 5 and 10. The closer to perfect you would have to be to feel really good about yourself, the closer to 10 you would place the X. If you feel satisfied with below average performance, then you would put an X over a number between 5 and 0.

Please read each question carefully. Take your time to think about each question, and then tell how well you need to do to be absolutely satisfied with yourself.

1. How popular do you have to be to feel really good about (absolutely satisfied with) yourself?

```
 0    1    2    3    4    5    6    7    8    9   10
 I don't care if anyone likes me          The most popular person in school
```

2. How good do your grades have to be to feel really good about (absolutely satisfied with) yourself?

```
 0    1    2    3    4    5    6    7    8    9   10
 0%   30%  40%  50%  60%  70%  75%  80%  85%  90% 100%
 I can fail everything    All C's                    All A's
```

3. How good-looking do you have to be to feel really good about (absolutely satisfied with) yourself?

```
 0    1    2    3    4    5    6    7    8    9   10
 Ugly                    Average              Like a model
```

4. How smart do you have to be . . . .

```
 0    1    2    3    4    5    6    7    8    9   10
 Stupid                  Average                   Genius
```

5. How well behaved do you have to be . . .

```
 0    1    2    3    4    5    6    7    8    9    10
 I can do everything wrong        Average       Never do anything wrong
```

6. How athletic (good at sports) do you have to be . . .

```
 0    1    2    3    4    5    6    7    8    9    10
 A complete klutz                                 A super star
```

7. How good-looking and fashionable do your clothes need to be . . .

```
 0    1    2    3    4    5    6    7    8    9    10
 Ragged & dirty           OK              Right out of a fashion
                                                        magazine
```

8. How funny do you have to be to feel really good. . . .

```
 0    1    2    3    4    5    6    7    8    9    10
 No sense of humor           Average           A comedian
```

9. How nice do you have to be to feel . . .

```
 0    1    2    3    4    5    6    7    8    9    10
 Meanest person             Average           Nicest person
```

10. How good must your possessions (things like money, jewelry, bicycle, toys, records, stereo, etc.) be in order to feel . . .

```
 0    1    2    3    4    5    6    7    8    9    10
 The worst                  Average              The best
```

PART 2

Please read the next ten questions and answer them according to how well your *parents* think you ought to do or to be in each of the following areas. As you did in Part 1 with the number scale, show how well your parents think you should do or be on each question.

1. How popular do you have to be to feel really good about (absolutely satisfied with) yourself?

```
0    1    2    3    4    5    6    7    8    9    10
I don't care                              The most popular person
if anyone likes me                                     in school
```

2. How good do your grades have to be to feel really good about (absolutely satisfied with) yourself?

```
0    1    2    3    4    5    6    7    8    9    10
0%  30%  40%  50%  60%  70%  75%  80%  85%  90% 100%
I can fail everything       All C's                   All A's
```

3. How good-looking do you have to be to feel really good about (absolutely satisfied with) yourself?

```
0    1    2    3    4    5    6    7    8    9    10
Ugly                      Average              Like a model
```

4. How smart do you have to be . . .

```
0    1    2    3    4    5    6    7    8    9    10
Stupid                    Average                    Genius
```

5. How well behaved do you have to be . . .

```
0    1    2    3    4    5    6    7    8    9    10
I can do everything wrong  Average    Never do anything wrong
```

6. How athletic (good at sports) do you have to be . . .

```
0    1    2    3    4    5    6    7    8    9    10
A complete klutz                            A super star
```

7. How good-looking and fashionable do your clothes need to be . . .

```
0    1    2    3    4    5    6    7    8    9    10
Ragged & dirty            OK         Right out of a fashion
                                                  magazine
```

8. How funny do you have to be to feel really good . . .

```
 0    1    2    3    4    5    6    7    8    9    10
No sense of humor            Average              A comedian
```

9. How nice do you have to be to feel . . .

```
 0    1    2    3    4    5    6    7    8    9    10
Meanest person              Average             Nicest person
```

10. How good must your possessions (things like money, jewelry, bicycle, toys, records, stereo, etc.) be in order to feel . . .

```
 0    1    2    3    4    5    6    7    8    9    10
The worst                   Average               The best
```

PART 3

Please read the next ten questions and answer them according to how you are feeling about yourself RIGHT NOW. Remember that this set of questions refers to how you feel you really are now—not how you would *like* to be. Use numbers 1-10 to answer the questions. Use low numbers to mean you are very popular, very good, very smart, etc., and high numbers to mean you are very unpopular, very low in intelligence, very bad looking, and so forth.

1. How popular or unpopular are you?
2. How good are your grades?
3. How good-looking are you?
4. How smart are you?
5. How well-behaved are you?
6. How athletic are you?
7. How good-looking are your clothes?
8. How funny are you?
9. How nice are you?
10. How good are your possessions?

PART 4

Please rank in order the following 10 things according to how important each one is to you. For example, if having good looks is most important to you, put a 1 in the blank next to good looks. If nice possessions are least important to you, you would put a 10 in a the blank next to nice possessions. Again, please take your time to really think about each of the 10 things before assigning a number to one.

___ Popularity
___ Good grades
___ Good looks
___ Intelligence
___ Good behavior
___ Athletic
___ Good-looking and fashionable clothes
___ Funny
___ Nice
___ Nice possessions (money, toys, records, etc.)

Final Words

Children don't inherit standards and goals. Parents have only one opportunity to pass on standards and goals to their children. The few years of childhood pass quickly. During those years, children are malleable, receptive, open to parental instruction. Later, during the teen years and after, some may wander from God's way, exploring different standards. It is not uncommon for older teens, even if they have been taught God's laws and His grace, to wander from them for a season as they seek to establish in their own minds and hearts the truths they have been taught over the years. At some point they must own their faith for themselves. The wise parent will pray unceasingly, surrender all children to their heavenly Father, and trust God to work in them even through their wandering. Then the early years of training will pay their dividends!

Truth can indeed "rustproof" children against the corrosive notions eating at the human spirit. When children think truthfully about life, they will be able to evaluate experiences, solve problems, express themselves effectively, behave appropriately, and exercise self-control. But they can acquire these skills only if they know what truth is, where to find it, and how to use it.

There is no higher goal for Christian parents than to work toward the day when they can say, as did the apostle John, "I have no greater joy than to hear that my children are walking in the truth" (3 John 4).

Appendix

Charts for the Practice of Cognitive-Behavioral Competence Enhancement Interventions With Children[1]

Adapted from
Michael L. Bloomquist, Ph.D.
Division of Child and Adolescent Psychiatry
University of Minnesota

HOW DO YOU FEEL TODAY?

When I Feel Strong Negative Emotions

Directions: Fill out this chart whenever you feel a strong negative emotion. It's okay if you don't remember to write it down immediately, but try to fill it out that day. Please provide the information asked for in each column.

Date	Event. (*What happened to make you feel a strong negative emotion?*)	Label Feelings. (*What were your feelings?*)	How did your body feel? (*Describe breathing, muscles tensing, heart rate, etc.*)	What were your thoughts? (*What did you say to yourself inside?*)	What were your actions? (*What did you do?*)	Feeling Rating. (*1 represents slightly negative, 10 is extremely negative.*)

Strong Negative Feeling-Management Worksheet

Directions: The child and/or parent can complete this worksheet. Answer each question as it pertains to strong negative feelings. Fill out the worksheet while you are trying to cope with, or after you have coped with, strong negative feelings.

1. What event or problem is making me feel strong negative feelings?

   _____
   _____
   _____

2. What feeling(s) am I feeling now? (Look at "Feelings Vocabulary Chart" if needed.) _____

   _____

3. What are the body, thinking, and action signals that tell me I feel this way? _____

   _____

4. What am I going to do to cope with this feeling(s)? How will I reduce my tension and change my thoughts? How should I talk to myself? What action should I take? _____

   _____
   _____
   _____

5. (If Applicable) After I've calmed down, how can I solve the problem that made me have those feelings in the first place? What can I do to solve the problem? _____

   _____
   _____
   _____
   _____

Strong Negative Feeling-Management Rating

How well did I cope with my strong negative feelings (using 1–4 ratings below)? (Circle one.)

1	2	3	4
Didn't use strong feeling-management skills at all.	Tried to use strong feeling-management skills, but it didn't really work.	Tried hard, went through the strong feeling-management skills, but it didn't really work.	Tried hard, went through the strong feeling-management skills, and it worked.

Problem-Recognition Signals

External Signals

I. Facial Expressions
   A. Angry expressions
   B. Sad expressions
   C. Other expressions

II. Body Postures
   A. Aggressive body
   B. Withdrawn body
   C. Other body expressions

III. Words/Voice Tone
   A. Angry/hostile words
   B. Raised tone of voice
   C. Very low tone of voice
   D. Other words and tone of voice

Internal Signals

I. Thoughts
   A. About self
   B. About others
   C. About situation
   D. Other thoughts

II. Feelings
   A. Angry
   B. Sad
   C. Nervous
   D. Other feelings

III. Body
   A. Tense muscles
   B. Rapid heart rate
   C. Sweating
   D. Other body sensations

Problem-Solving Steps

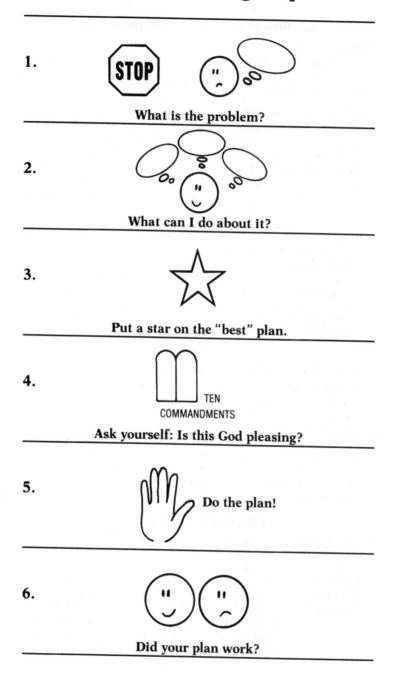

1.

What is the problem?

2.

What can I do about it?

3.

Put a star on the "best" plan.

4.

TEN
COMMANDMENTS

Ask yourself: Is this God pleasing?

5. **Do the plan!**

6.

Did your plan work?

Six-Step Problem-Solving Worksheet

Directions: The parent and/or child can complete this form. Answer each question as it pertains to the problem at hand. You can fill this out to solve a problem occuring at the moment or to figure out how you could have solved a problem better.

1. What is the problem? _____
   _____

2. What are some plans (solutions) that I could use? List as many plans (solutions) as I can think of. _____
   _____
   _____
   _____

3. What is the best plan? Think ahead about what would happen if I tried the plans in Step 2. After I think about each plan, decide which one will work best. _____
   _____
   _____

4. Is this pleasing to God? _____
   _____
   _____

5. Do the plan. How will I do the plan? What will I do to make the plan work? _____
   _____
   _____

6. Did the plan work? _____
   _____
   _____
   _____

Problem-Solving Rating

How well did I use problem-solving (using 1–4 ratings below)? (Circle one.)

1	2	3	4
Didn't use problem-solving at all.	Tried to use problem-solving a little, but it didn't really work.	Tried hard, went through the problem-solving steps, but didn't really use the best plan.	Tried hard, went through the problem-solving steps and used the best plan.

Means-End Problem-Solving Worksheet

Directions: The parent and/or child can complete this form. Answer each question as it pertains to the problem at hand. You can fill this out to solve a problem occuring at the moment or to figure out how you could have solved a problem better.

1. What is the goal? _____
   _____
   _____
   _____

2. What steps do I need to reach my goal?
   Step 1: _____
   _____
   _____

   Step 2: _____
   _____
   _____

   Step 3: _____
   _____
   _____

   Step 4: _____
   _____
   _____

3. Did I reach my goal? (Answer this question after all above steps have been completed.) _____
   _____
   _____
   _____
   _____

Problem-Solving Rating

How well did I use problem-solving (using 1–4 ratings below)? (Circle one.)

1	2	3	4
Didn't use problem-solving at all.	Tried to use problem-solving a little, but it didn't really work.	Tried hard, went through the problem-solving steps, but didn't really use the best plan.	Tried hard, went through the problem-solving steps and used the best plan.

Practicing Social Skills

Before Social Event

1. I will work on (state specific social behavior): _____

   _____

   _____

2. When and where I will work on the social behavior (designate time and place): _____

   _____

   _____

   _____

After Social Event

3. How well did I do? (circle one)

1	2	3	4	5
Not at All Good	A Little Good	Okay	Pretty Good	Great

4. What did I do that tells me how to rate myself? (write down how you know you deserve the above rating): _____

   _____

   _____

5. If my parent(s) agree with my rating and it is a 3, 4, or 5, I get this reward: _____

   _____

   _____

Directions: The parent(s) and/or child can complete the form, but all involved should discuss it. Complete Steps 1 and 2 before the event and Steps 3, 4, and 5 after the social event.

Family Problem-Solving Worksheet

Directions: The family completes this form together as they attempt to solve a problem. Answer each question as it pertains to the problem.

1. What is the problem we are having? Decide as a family what the problem is and write it down. _____
   _____
   _____

2. What are some plans we could use? Write down as many plans as you can think of. Let each family member have input. ____
   _____
   _____
   _____

3. What is the best plan we could use? Select the plan that will most likely work and make most family members feel okay. Write down the plan the family has decided to use. _____
   _____
   _____
   _____

4. Is this pleasing to God? _____
   _____
   _____

5. Do the plan. Write down exactly what the family did when using the plan. _____
   _____
   _____

6. Did the plan work? Write down how you know if a plan worked or not. _____
   _____
   _____
   _____

Family Problem-Solving Rating

How well did we use problem-solving (using 1–4 ratings below)? (Circle one.)

1	2	3	4
We didn't use family problem-solving at all.	We tried to use family problem-solving, but it didn't really work.	We tried hard, went through the family problem-solving steps, but didn't really use the plan.	We tried hard, went through the family problem-solving steps and used the best plan.

A special thank you to those who contributed to interviews and questionnaires. Their help was invaluable.

Cindy Alewine
Mocha Backus
Anne Barber
Vicki Bomgren
Jerry Brown
Sharon Brown
Sharon Chalgren
Diane Dahlen
Traci DePree
Sharon Erickson
Edie Gates
Joyce Hardwick
Carol Johnson
Amanda Kamla
Patricia Lien

Sharon Madison
Beth Michaelson
Jeanne Mikkelson
Jan Shepley
Carol Starr
Jacob Templeton
Jennifer Templeton
Morris Vaagenes
Bonnie Vaagenes
Sherry Wiese
Steve Wiese
Kathy Wood
Nancy Wright
Lance Wubbels

Notes

Introduction:

1. Saint Augustine, *The City of God*, translated by Marcus Dods (New York: Random House, 1950).

2. See 1 Corinthians 2:6-16

3. 2 Corinthians 1:20.

4. William Backus and Marie Chapian, *Telling Yourself the Truth* (Minneapolis: Bethany House Publishers, 1980).

5. Deuteronomy 6:6, 7.

Chapter 5:

1. Saint Augustine, *The City of God*, tr. Marcus Dods (New York: Random House, 1950), p. 452ff. In this fascinating passage, Saint Augustine sets forth the important distinction between truthful (rational) emotions (affections) and those based on misbeliefs. He further distinguishes between the stoic ideal of *apatheia* (emotionlessness) and the biblical ideal of appropriate expression of emotions based on truth. Contemporary cognitive psychology as we understand it and expound it in this book was

anticipated more than 1500 years ago.

2. Kevin D. Stark, *Childhood Depression: School-based Intervention* (New York: Guilford Press, 1990), pp. 111–114.

3. *Ibid.*

Chapter 6:

1. Kevin D. Stark, *Childhood Depression: School-based Intervention* (New York: Guilford Press, 1990).

2. *Ibid.*, p. 126.

3. If you want to be more fully informed about how to use powerful rewards in training children, work through our book *Empowering Parents* (Minneapolis: Bethany House Publishers, 1992).

4. Hannah Whitall Smith, *The Christian's Secret of a Happy Life* (Old Tappan, N.J.: Revell, 1942), p. 57.

Chapter 9:

1. Eugene H. Methvin, "How To Hold A Riot," *National Review* (June 8, 1992), pp. 32–35.

2. For some of the material in this chapter, we are indebted to Eva L. Feindler for her excellent chapter in Philip Kendall, ed., *Child and Adolescent Therapy: Cognitive-Behavioral Procedures* (New York: Guilford Press, 1991).

Chapter 10:

1. Aesop, from *Book Trails: Through the Wildwood*, ed. Renée B. Stern and O. Muriel Fuller (Chicago: Shepard and Lawrence, 1928).

Chapter 11:

1. Pope, McHale, and Craighead, *Self-Esteem Enhancement with Children and Adolescents* (Elmsford, N.Y.: Pergamon Press, 1988).

Chapter 12:

1. Alice W. Pope, Susan M. McHale, and W. Edward Craighead, *Self-Esteem Enhancement With Children and Adolescents* (Elmsford, N.Y.: Pergamon Press, 1988).

2. Michael Bloomquist, *Charts for the Practice of Cognitive-Behavioral Competence Enhancement Interventions With Children* (distributed at a workshop by Dr. Bloomquist with note: "Workshop participants have permission to reproduce and/or modify these charts"). We have modified these materials.

Chapter 13:

1. James C. Dobson, *Parenting Isn't for Cowards* (Waco, Tex.: Word, 1987), p. 144.

2. Lauren Braswell, Michael Bloomquist, and Sheila Peterson, *A Guide to Understanding and Helping With Attention Deficit Hyperactivity Disorder in School Settings* (Minneapolis: Department of Professional Development, University of Minnesota).

3. Kevin D. Stark, *Childhood Depression: School-based Intervention* (New York: Guilford Press, 1990).

Appendix

1. Lauren Braswell, Michael Bloomquist, and Sheila Peterson, *A Guide to Understanding and Helping With Attention Deficit Hyperactivity Disorder in School Settings* (Minneapolis: Department of Professional Development, University of Minnesota).